THE SECOND EPISTLE OF PAUL
TO THE CORINTHIANS

An Exposition

THE
SECOND EPISTLE
OF PAUL
TO
THE CORINTHIANS

An Exposition

by
CHARLES R. ERDMAN

PREFACE BY EARL F. ZEIGLER

THE WESTMINSTER PRESS
PHILADELPHIA

Published by The Westminster Press®
Philadelphia, Pennsylvania

PRINTED IN THE UNITED STATES OF AMERICA

To
My Brother
Frederick Erdman
the beloved physician
whose ministry to bodies and to souls
has been marvelously blessed

PREFACE

The apostle Paul had enormous capacity as a writer. Witness the number of New Testament books credited to him. Someone has estimated that II Corinthians, had it been typed double space on 8½″ x 11″ sheets, about three hundred words per page, would have filled twenty pages—about six thousand words. When the church in Corinth received this "book," some time would be needed for it to be read publicly and slowly, and much more time for it to be discussed and to reach decisions that Paul anticipated.

The preparation of expositions of an apostle of Paul's versatility and authority requires a dedicated, scholarly, and warmhearted writer. All these characteristics and many more were combined in Dr. Charles R. Erdman, who was selected to write the seventeen volumes that comprise the Erdman series of New Testament commentaries. A good expositor must study a book like II Corinthians in the original Greek. He then will live with the letter until its message speaks to him in no uncertain tongue. In imagination he will dwell in Corinth and mingle with the inhabitants and visitors until he knows their thinking and practices which, in the case of ancient Corinth, often were not commendable. He will worship with the infant church in the home of some member, and listen without comment as he hears Paul's letter read and discussed. Then he will return to the present to formulate an outline of the letter to provide the student of today with a guide to Paul's thinking. Then the expositor will be ready to explain the letter section by section. Early in ch. 1:8-11 he will come across reference to some crushing and almost deadly experience that Paul suffered in Asia. This will require research to provide the present-day student with reliable "options" on what the apostle may have meant. The expositor may decide to explain how he "voted" and why. Throughout the letter the expositor will be compelled to say many times that "we have no certain knowledge on this or that reference, but it may mean so and so." The problem of the expositor is made more complex by lack of information concerning the exact situation to which Paul may be writing. But instead of "mixing up" the student, a good expositor leads him through the labyrinth to light and to a satisfying conclusion. The interpreter knows that the student is interested in more than an understanding of ancient church history. He wants to know the contemporary message. Often he would not discover it on his own, but an expositor like Dr. Erdman leads the student to admit, "This has relevance for me and my age." This is the primary objective in Bible study—to make its message come alive now.

Dr. Charles R. Erdman was a professor of practical theology in Princeton Theological Seminary, as well as pastor of three thriving churches prior to becoming and while a professor. His commentaries are very practical, and lay and ministerial men and women for decades have profited from Dr. Erdman's tutelage. This paperback edition, printed from entirely new type and plates, will continue to preach the word in season and out of season to this generation whom our world needs as witnesses.

FOREWORD

This passionate letter presents a fascinating and profound philosophy of life. Its phrases are measured by the throbbings of a great heroic heart. The author appears as the exemplar and defender of the noblest ideals and the supreme privileges of the Christian ministry, while his human weakness, his sincerity, his struggles, and his tears evoke our sympathy, our admiration, and our love. His message impresses upon every reader the priceless value of loyal friendships, the imperishable influence of unselfish service, and the incomparable glory and power of the gospel of Christ.

INTRODUCTION

This epistle was written by Paul to the Christians in Corinth to prepare them for his approaching visit. He was on his third missionary journey. After a protracted stay in Ephesus, he was passing through Macedonia to Greece. Possibly at Philippi he met his messenger, Titus, who brought tidings from the Corinthian church. These were of such a character as to make necessary the following letter, with which Titus was sent back to Corinth. He was to carry out certain instructions of the apostle and to announce his near approach.

Paul had founded the church some five years before, when on his second missionary journey. It was this journey which resulted in bringing the gospel from Asia to Europe, and the Corinthian church was possibly the most abiding monument of that memorable tour. The essential feature of his third journey was the sojourn of more than two years in Ephesus. During this time Paul was in constant communication with his friends at Corinth across the Aegean Sea. His heart was burdened continually by reports of the perils by which the infant church was threatened. To correct certain abuses and in reply to specific questions, he had written the letter which is known as First Corinthians, and now, on his way to revisit the city, he addresses to the church this important epistle which is known as Second Corinthians. From references contained in both of these letters it appears, however, that Paul made more than these two visits to Corinth and that he wrote at least two other letters to this church. Some knowledge of these incidents in the life of Paul is necessary to a full understanding of this second epistle. It must be confessed, however, that a satisfactory reconstruction of the history is difficult, if not impossible. This is not because of the lack, but of the abundance, of the historic material. The endeavor brings one to what an eminent expositor has called "a trackless forest." The problem becomes tangled because, while the details appear rather definite, it proves baffling to search for any one unquestioned course of events which includes them all. However, they all belong to the limited period of Paul's two years at Ephesus and the main features of the story are not difficult to record.

It appears certain that at least one letter was dispatched by Paul to Corinth (I Cor. 5:9) before he wrote what is known as First Corinthians. It would seem further that between First and Second Corinthians at least one other letter was sent. This is described as a sorrowful letter, written with anguish of heart and with many tears. (II Cor. 2:3-4.) Paul even regretted for a time that it had been penned (ch. 7:8); yet under the influence of Titus, its bearer, a happy effect had been produced. It seems hardly possible to identify this letter with First Corinthians. The latter does contain certain stern paragraphs; but its spirit is calm, its emotions are controlled, and its evident purpose is to instruct rather than to rebuke.

It seems further that Paul paid to Corinth a brief, painful, unrecorded visit, which some students place before the writing of his first epistle. This is now more commonly supposed to have taken place between the time of the first and the second of the epistles which have been preserved (II Cor. 2:1; 12:14; 13:1).

Still further it would appear that Paul had promised a speedy visit, which he was to make by coming directly across the Aegean. Consequently the Corinthians were disappointed because of his delay, and because he was actually coming by way of Macedonia, which course, however, was according to the plan clearly stated in his first epistle (I Cor. 16:5; II Cor. 1:15).

It therefore may be conjectured that after the writing of his first epistle conditions in the church became more serious, demanding of Paul a speedy voyage across the sea to Corinth. On this brief visit his forbearance was mistaken for weakness. He was subjected to actual humiliation and left abruptly for Ephesus, promising to return soon. From Ephesus he wrote the sorrowful and painful letter of severe rebuke relating his changed plan of travel. Aided by the influence of Titus, the Corinthian offenders repented with deep contrition. The abuses in the church were corrected. Confidence in the apostle was fully restored. In accordance with Paul's instructions, Titus started on his journey toward Ephesus by way of Macedonia. Meanwhile Paul's long stay at Ephesus had been brought to an end. He set out for Corinth, but by the longer route, expecting to meet Titus at Troas, with news from Corinth. In spite of the wide door for evangelistic work open before him at Troas, Paul pressed on to Macedonia. There at last he met Titus, whose favorable report thrilled his heart with overwhelming joy. He learned that the great body of Corinthian Christians had obeyed his command and had shown toward him their deep affection and their devoted loyalty. However, they had neglected to complete the offering which he had requested of them for the needy Judean Christians. Then, too, there were among them certain false apostles who denied Paul's authority and tried to brand him as a mercenary impostor.

Paul now explains the change in his plans and the reason for delaying his visit. He expresses his confidence in the Corinthian Christians and his tender love for them. He dwells at length upon the sincere, devoted, glorious, accredited character of his ministry. He urges them to complete before his arrival the contribution for the suffering saints in Jerusalem. He sternly rebukes his unscrupulous adversaries. He exposes their intrigue and deceit. He shows the absurdity of their claims, vindicates completely his position as an apostle of Christ, and warns his opponents of the severe discipline he will administer when he comes again if they persist in their hostile and wicked conduct.

Such an attempted reconstruction of the circumstances attending the writing of this epistle at least makes evident the main elements in the problem. It presents the chief points of historic interest in the movements of Paul and indicates that a more exact knowledge of his experiences would throw further light upon his recorded words.

It should be insisted, however, that the uncertainty surrounding the movements of the writer in no way affects the understanding of those great spiritual truths which, though quite incidentally, he sets forth; nor does it in any wise make difficult the practical application of these truths to the problems of modern life.

Here, as plainly as in his other epistles, great fundamental doctrines are discerned. Here is revealed the glory of the exalted Christ, his reconciling work, and his transforming power. Here is declared the duty of service and of strict avoidance of sin. Here is the assurance of pardon and the promise that present experiences of grace will issue in a life of celestial glory.

However, this letter is less doctrinal than any of the other epistles, with the exception of Philemon. Its teachings produce deeper conviction because introduced casually and as matters of course. Furthermore, the artless introduction of historic incidents and the perplexing array of personal references demonstrate the genuineness of the letter and make it by far the most biographical of all the writings of the great apostle. The difficulty of arranging in satisfactory sequence these personal references only adds to the impression of genuineness.

Yet it is not the events of his outward life which attract our supreme interest. It is rather the revelation which is here made of the apostle's soul. We look into his very heart. We see his motives, his anguish, his joys, his fears, his hopes, his wounded feelings, his ardent love. Evidently the whole letter was written under the stress of strong emotion. It is this fact, rather than the uncertainty of the personal references, which makes portions of the epistle difficult to understand. The style is broken, involved, and at times obscure. The impetuosity of the thought moves from point to point with a rapidity which makes it hard to grasp the sequence and connection. Much is indicated as beneath the surface. It is a question how far some statements are ironical, or how far they are to be taken as expressions of facts.

The language is picturesque. It abounds in metaphors which are frequently embodied in single words. The epistle is one of many moods. "Joy and heaviness, anxiety and hope, trust and resentment, anger and love" follow one another with bewildering abruptness. It presents a conflict of feelings in which gratitude and indignation, gladness and grief, are struggling for the mastery. Mingled severity and tenderness, reproof and praise, command and exhortation, suffering and rejoicing, humiliation and exaltation, are set forth in terms unparalleled in all the literature of the world. "Ecstatic thanksgiving and cutting irony, self-assertion and self-abnegation, condemnation and warning, authority, paradox, and apology, all meet and cross and seethe; yet out of the swirling eddies rise like rocks grand Christian principles and inspiring hopes."

Amid all the storm of passion Paul is ever under perfect self-control. The circumstances explain and justify it all. He is ever the master of himself, sincere, intelligent, consistent. The great truths of Christian experience are made the more striking because of the surroundings in which they appear; and even the humblest duties are enforced by reference to the highest laws. In fact, "a new philosophy of life is poured forth, not through systematic treatises, but through bursts of human feeling."

Whatever the seeming difficulty of statement, whatever the obscurity of historic reference, Paul's majestic personality stands forth in this epistle, clearly revealed. His limitations are nowhere more obvious; but his heroic greatness never appears more supreme. Yet all his virtues, his excellencies, and his glory are evident reflections of an unseen Person in whose presence he is standing. The secret of his life is laid bare, his one impelling purpose is made plain, as we hear him passionately declare, "The love of Christ constraineth us; because we thus judge, that one died for all, therefore all died; and he died for all, that they that live should no longer live unto themselves, but unto him who for their sakes died and rose again."

THE OUTLINE

I

I
PAUL'S PRINCIPLES
OF ACTION
II Cor. 1:1 to 7:16

A. THE SALUTATION   Ch. 1:1-2

1 Paul, an apostle of Christ Jesus through the will of God, and Timothy our brother, unto the church of God which is at Corinth, with all the saints that are in the whole of Achaia: 2 Grace to you and peace from God our Father and the Lord Jesus Christ.

The name of Paul, placed at the beginning of a book, arrests the attention of the reader. This man stands supreme among the followers of Christ. To him more than to any other is due the extension of Christianity from Jerusalem to Rome, and the subsequent advance of Christian civilization into every region of the world.

In this place the name Paul is not a forgery. It is not assumed by a writer to attract attention to his work. No document from the distant centuries is more certainly authoritative. Not even the epistle to the Galatians is more surely a product of the great apostle. The artless profusion of personal references makes this a veritable chapter in the life of Paul. This is the first source of its fascination and its charm. Here are recorded not only the most dramatic incidents in a distinguished career, but the actual motives, the impulses, the struggles, the yearnings, of a great human heart.

Paul had recently passed through one of the most fruitful periods followed by one of the most painful experiences of his life. For more than two years he had been working

in Ephesus. A great Christian community had been established. The whole province of Asia had been evange-
lized. Letters had been written for the instruction of distant churches. Plans had been formulated for a journey
to Rome. Soon after, the apostle had narrowly escaped
from deadly violence; his heart had been crushed by dis-
appointing news from Corinth; and he had been tortured
by the delay of his messenger Titus. Now at last good
tidings have come. Titus has brought a favorable report
from the Corinthian church; and from some point in Macedonia, Paul is writing this letter to express his gratification,
to encourage gifts for needy Christians in Jerusalem, and
to rebuke certain enemies who are questioning his apostolic authority.

Therefore, when he styles himself "an apostle of Christ
Jesus through the will of God," he is coming to the very
heart of his epistle, and is striking one of the notes which
he finds it necessary to prolong. The phrase is familiar,
yet it gains significance from the closing chapters of this
letter, and in any connection it is full of meaning. "An
apostle" is a messenger. The term means literally "one
who is sent." It is fairly rendered by the modern word
"missionary." Incidentally, it is well to be reminded that
this is a missionary message, sent by the world's greatest
missionary to a missionary church; and in the light of such
facts the letter should be read.

The term "apostle" had acquired a technical sense. It
denoted one who had been commissioned by Christ, who
was a witness of the resurrection, and who had the credentials of miraculous powers. Thus Paul here calls himself
"an apostle of Christ Jesus," by which he means that
Christ Jesus appointed him to his office. This appointment, he claimed, was by means of a heavenly vision and
not by any agency of man. He here further declares it
to have been in accordance with a divine purpose, and
"through the will of God."

In some real, if secondary, sense all Christians are mes-

sengers or missionaries of Christ Jesus. "Through the will
of God" they are sent forth as those who have been divinely called into the service of Christ. They belong to
Christ and the substance of all their witness, by word or
by deed, is to be the truth concerning his divine person
and his redeeming work.

In these introductory phrases Paul unites with his own
name that of Timothy. Of all persons in the world
Timothy was most precious to the heart of Paul. He had
become a Christian under Paul's influence when the apostle was at Lystra on his second missionary journey. Since
then he had been Paul's closest companion. By his own
presence and preaching he had aided in establishing the
church at Corinth. More recently he had planned a visit
to that church. It is not certain that he carried out this
purpose, but in any event he was now with Paul in Macedonia. His disposition was rather timid and retiring; but
he was not lacking in ability, in vigor, or in moral courage.
His sincerity and sympathy won the affection of Paul, who
elsewhere calls him his "true child," and testifies that his
service had been "like a son to a father."

Here Paul is careful not to call him an apostle, but
designates him as "our brother." By this title he refers
to the brotherhood of Christian believers who constitute
the most notable fraternity in all history. The purpose
here is not to emphasize the relation of Timothy to Paul,
but the relation to Timothy to the readers of the epistle.
It is not intimated that he is aiding Paul in composing
the letter, or even that he is writing it as Paul's amanuensis.
Rather, it is intimated that what is written by the apostle
has the approval of a fellow Christian who is held by the
readers in brotherly affection and high esteem.

The readers are described as constituting "the church
of God which is at Corinth." That was a strange place
in which to find a church of God. The city was noted
for its immorality, its license, and its pagan impurity; but
there the power of the gospel had been demonstrated by

the establishment of a flourishing society of redeemed souls. This church, it is true, had its great perils and its faults. These pressed as a heavy burden on the heart of Paul. Once and again he had found it necessary to admonish and rebuke these immature believers; now he is writing to them with deep affection, not only as to converts whom he has brought to Christ, but as to a brotherhood which has been brought into being by God and is the object of his love and care.

With these Christians, Paul unites, in his salutation, all their fellow believers who "are in the whole of Achaia." He refers to the Roman province which is practically identical with modern Greece. In this region there were many scattered converts, as at Cenchreae and Athens. Paul does not mean that he is composing a circular letter to be sent to a number of neighboring churches, but rather that he has in mind all believers who are in communication with the church at Corinth. He designates them as "saints." This had become already a common name for all Christians. During the earthly life of their Master they had been known as "disciples," and subsequently they called themselves "brethren"; but Paul more commonly described them as "saints." The word did not denote moral perfection but the high privilege and objective and destiny of those who, as the result of a divine call, were holy, separated unto God; those who, as his people, were expected to keep themselves from sin and to serve his Son.

To these readers Paul addresses his apostolic salutation, "Grace to you and peace from God our Father and the Lord Jesus Christ." Some personal greeting was usual at the opening of a Greek letter; but Paul transforms a common courtesy into a spiritual appeal. He expresses his wish, indeed his prayer, that his readers may be granted grace and peace. This was a common form of Oriental salutation, and for centuries peace had been united with grace in the benediction of the Jewish priests, "Jehovah . . . be gracious unto thee: . . . and give thee peace."

However, Paul fills both familiar terms with new and larger meaning.   Grace denotes the free and unmerited favor of God, and is in itself the source and origin of peace, which in its turn is meant to include all those spiritual blessings which God can bestow.   Paul asks that these may be supplied by God, in his relation to believers as their heavenly Father, and by Jesus Christ, whom they acknowledge as their Lord.   Such an implied equality of "God our Father" and "the Lord Jesus Christ" is surprising even to many modern readers, but it is a witness to the faith of the early church, shared by believers in all the succeeding centuries, that God is bestowing all his gracious gifts through the divine Person of his Son, our Savior and our Lord.

B. THE THANKSGIVING   Ch. 1:3-11

3 Blessed be *the God and Father of our Lord Jesus Christ, the Father of mercies and God of all comfort;   4 who comforteth us in all our affliction, that we may be able to comfort them that are in any affliction, through the comfort wherewith we ourselves are comforted of God.   5 For as the sufferings of Christ abound unto us, even so our comfort also aboundeth through Christ.   6 But whether we are afflicted, it is for your comfort and salvation; or whether we are comforted, it is for your comfort, which worketh in the patient enduring of the same sufferings which we also suffer: 7 and our hope for you is stedfast; knowing that, as ye are partakers of the sufferings, so also are ye of the comfort.   8 For we would not have you ignorant, brethren, concerning our affliction which befell* us *in Asia, that we were weighed down exceedingly, beyond our power, insomuch that we despaired even of life: 9 yea, we ourselves have had the sentence of death within ourselves, that we should not trust in ourselves, but in God who raiseth the dead: 10 who delivered us out of so great a death, and will deliver: on whom we have set our hope that he will also still deliver us;   11 ye also helping together on our behalf by your supplication; that, for the gift be-*

stowed upon us by means of many, thanks may be given by many persons on our behalf.

It is common to find an expression of thanksgiving added to the opening salutation, in the secular letters of Paul's day. With the apostle the practice was so invariable that the omission of an opening thanksgiving in his epistle to the Galatians places a startling emphasis upon the stern rebuke with which that letter begins. Usually Paul returns thanks for spiritual graces which God has conferred upon the readers. In Second Corinthians, as in First Timothy, the gratitude expressed is for benefits he has himself received. However, the persons addressed are very definitely in his mind. The divine bestowals upon Paul are said to have as their ultimate purpose the comfort and encouragement of his readers, and these very gifts are regarded by the apostle as answers to their prayers.

He expresses two reasons for thanksgiving. First, he gives thanks for divine comfort (vs. 3-7), and second, for divine deliverance (vs. 8-11). In each case the apostle has in mind some deadly peril in which he has been afforded consolation and courage, and out of which he has been delivered by the power of God.

He ascribes all praise, all thanksgiving, all glory, to God: "Blessed be the God and Father of our Lord Jesus Christ, the Father of mercies and God of all comfort." There is something rather surprising in speaking of the God of our Lord Jesus Christ. Yet, with all the mystery involved, it is proper to speak not only of the Christ of God but of the God of Christ. Here our Lord is mentioned as the Channel and Agent through whom all blessings are communicated to men. The blessings here particularly in view are those of compassion and comfort. Therefore, God is described as "the Father of mercies," or the compassionate Father, and "the God of all comfort."

Ten times do these first five verses make mention of comfort. Their rhythmic cadences form a veritable hymn of consolation. Their message is such as to inspire hope in every sorrowing heart. Their summons is to the service of others, by kindly sympathy, by encouragement, and by the gracious ministry of good cheer.

The comfort here specially in mind is that which comes to one who is suffering as a follower of Christ. It is specifically the comfort of an apostle who has been sharing the sufferings of his Lord. Yet the notes of this song of cheer may strike responsive chords in the soul of anyone who feels the burden of affliction or the burning desire to bring relief to those who are in need.

True comfort is traced to its divine Source. In view of the consolation he has himself received, Paul would ascribe thanksgiving and praise and blessing to the "God of all comfort." Here for the first time in the New Testament God is described as a divine Comforter. In his farewell discourse Christ so described himself, when he declared that his abiding Spirit was to be for his followers "another Comforter." Christ had been a true Comforter to his disciples and henceforth his Spirit was to continue his blessed work. The word "comforter" or "paraclete" is very beautiful. It describes one who is called to the side of another to give help. This help may be in the nature of cheer, courage, or new strength. Such help Paul had found in a time of desperate need, and he ascribes it to "the Father who is full of compassion," to "the God who is the giver of all comfort."

The means by which the comfort was given Paul does not state. In the case of other Christians it comes sometimes by the reading of Scripture, sometimes by the sympathetic ministries of friends, sometimes by the removal of the affliction, sometimes by the secret offices of the divine Spirit. But, whatever the method, Paul traces the source of relief to the loving heart of God.

The apostle declares further that God has a definite purpose in imparting his consolation. It is, "that we may be able to comfort them that are in any affliction, through the comfort wherewith we ourselves are comforted of God." Probably it is an exaggeration to assert that one who has never suffered is powerless to bring consolation or help or cheer. An angel brought strength to Christ in the hour of his agony, and yet angels do not suffer. However, one who has endured pain and anguish is more likely to sympathize with suffering; and surely those who have found divine comfort in times of affliction are the ones best qualified to bring others who are afflicted to the same Source of strength, and to share with them the consolation which has brought peace and courage to their own souls.

Paul adds that his consolation, even as his suffering, was due to his relation to Christ, "for as the sufferings of Christ abound unto us, even so our comfort also aboundeth through Christ."

By this reference to "the sufferings of Christ" Paul did not claim any part in the unique, atoning, redeeming work of the divine Savior. Yet he meant more than that his sufferings were endured for the sake of Christ. He meant that the opposition, the persecution, the cruelties he endured were like those which Christ endured, and that he submitted to them as a servant of Christ, and as one who by faith was identified with Christ. If, then, in virtue of this vital union, he had an abundant share in the sufferings of his Lord, he was sure that through the same union with Christ he was receiving an abundant supply of divine comfort. The same unfailing confidence can be shared by all the followers of Christ. Those who are willing to suffer with their Lord, who consent to take up the cross as his followers, can be sure of his consolation and his strength.

While Paul is thus expressing gratitude for the divine comfort which he himself is enjoying, his thought is actually centering upon the Corinthian Christians to whom this letter is addressed. They are the ultimate recipients of all the grace vouchsafed to him. So he adds, "But whether we are afflicted, it is for your comfort and salvation; or whether we are comforted, it is for your com-

fort, which worketh in the patient enduring of the same
sufferings which we also suffer." Therefore, both his sufferings and his comfort benefit those to whom he is writing. The skill which he acquires in the school of affliction
enables him so to comfort those who endure similar trials
that their faith is strengthened, their patience is made more
steadfast, their salvation is assured.

The purpose of suffering has never been fully revealed.
Its mystery still remains. However, one of its blessed
results is the ability it gives to soothe and sympathize,
to cheer and to strengthen others, when in his own suffering a man has experienced the presence and the comfort
of God. Therefore Paul can close his thanksgiving for
the consolation he has received with a statement which is
truly complimentary to his friends in Corinth. He affirms
his absolute confidence that they are partaking both of the
sufferings of Christ and of the comfort of Christ.

How real and how deadly his own sufferings have been,
Paul now sets forth, as in the four closing verses of his
thanksgiving he expresses his gratitude for divine deliverance.

What was the exact peril from which he had been rescued, it is impossible to discover. Some have conjectured
that it was a shipwreck; but such could hardly be described as having been "in Asia." This phrase probably
denotes Ephesus, the great Asiatic capital, which had been
for three years the scene of his struggles and his success.
Many believe that the reference here is to the intolerable
suffering Paul endured when he learned of the rebellion
and divisions in the Corinthian church, and when he was
informed of the attacks made upon him by the enemies
who denied his authority, questioned his integrity, and attempted to destroy his work. Undoubtedly this was one
of the most crushing blows which ever fell upon this devoted servant of Christ. It is true also that deliverance
from this distress by the good news from Corinth was the
very occasion of the epistle, and that reference to such

deliverance would be pertinent in this introductory thanks-giving. Yet it would appear that the language here employed is rather extravagant if descriptive of mental depression resulting from evil tidings, however severe that depression may have been.

Others suppose that Paul's peril was that of a severe illness which had brought him into the very shadow and despair of certain death. However, such an experience would scarcely be classed among "the sufferings of Christ." Of course one may bear sickness with heroic courage for the sake of Christ and by the grace of Christ; but Christ's sufferings were rather those of opposition and persecution due to the malice and hatred of men. They were not of the nature of bodily disease.

It is quite possible that Paul referred to some unrecorded outbreak of fury and violence from which escape seemed absolutely hopeless. This was not the uproar and riot caused by Demetrius, with the account of which The Acts closes the story of Paul's stay in Ephesus. Special mention is made of the safety of the apostle on that particular occasion. However, such a scene indicates what may have occurred afterward. Paul declared in his first epistle to the Corinthians that during his stay at Ephesus he had "fought with beasts." By this he referred probably to the opposition and violence of brutal and bestial men. Such men may have inflicted great suffering upon the apostle.

Whatever the specific peril may have been, it was surely extraordinary and unique even among the tragic and tempestuous and thrilling experiences of Paul. By it he was "prostrated beyond all power of endurance." He was without any way of escape, was "utterly at a loss." He actually despaired of life. Indeed, when he asked himself the question whether the issue was to be life or death, the only possible answer was death.

For deliverance from such imminent peril Paul is returning thanks; but he pauses to express the purpose of

God in allowing him to come to such a place of hopeless-
ness. It was that Paul might be stripped of all self-confidence and inspired with a new trust in God. As the apostle declares, "We ourselves have had the sentence of death
within ourselves, that we should not trust in ourselves, but
in God who raiseth the dead." Thus he came to have a
new confidence in God as able not only to keep from
death, but to raise from the dead. Thus, in this bitterest
experience Paul had ever known, he found faith born of
despair.

Such faith gave birth in turn to imperishable hope, so
that he could refer to God as the One "who delivered us
out of so great a death, and will deliver: on whom we have
set our hope that he will also still deliver us."

To God, then, Paul is grateful for so signal a deliverance; yet in his expression of thanks he is never unmindful
of the friends to whom his letter is addressed. In fact, he
closes his thanksgiving with a beautiful reference in which
he ascribes to them a part, and a very real part, in his res-
cue from death. They had been "helping together" by
their prayers on his behalf. In their petitions and in God's
gracious reply there had been a divine purpose. It was
that, when the deliverance came, Paul should not be alone
in giving thanks. The many who had prayed for him
would, with upturned faces, give thanks on his behalf.

Thus, in the opening thanksgiving of his epistle, Paul
expresses his confidence in the Corinthian Christians and
in their deep concern for him. He pictures the true communion of believers: Those who find divine comfort rejoice that they are fitted thus to become ministers of consolation; those who are granted divine deliverance unite
in thanksgiving with those whose prayers have been in-
strumental in their relief. Thus all are united in new gratitude toward "the Father of mercies and God of all comfort."

C. THE EXPLANATION   Chs. 1:12 to 2:11

1. THE CHANGED PLAN   Ch. 1:12-22

12 For our glorying is this, the testimony of our conscience, that in holiness and sincerity of God, not in fleshly wisdom but in the grace of God, we behaved ourselves in the world, and more abundantly to you-ward. 13 For we write no other things unto you, than what ye read or even acknowledge, and I hope ye will acknowledge unto the end: 14 as also ye did acknowledge us in part, that we are your glorying, even as ye also are ours, in the day of our Lord Jesus.

15 And in this confidence I was minded to come first unto you, that ye might have a second benefit; 16 and by you to pass into Macedonia, and again from Macedonia to come unto you, and of you to be set forward on my journey unto Judæa. 17 When I therefore was thus minded, did I show fickleness? or the things that I purpose, do I purpose according to the flesh, that with me there should be the yea yea and the nay nay? 18 But as God is faithful, our word toward you is not yea and nay. 19 For the Son of God, Jesus Christ, who was preached among you by us, even by me and Silvanus and Timothy, was not yea and nay, but in him is yea. 20 For how many soever be the promises of God, in him is the yea: wherefore also through him is the Amen, unto the glory of God through us. 21 Now he that establisheth us with you in Christ, and anointed us, is God; 22 who also sealed us, and gave us the earnest of the Spirit in our hearts.

Occasionally it is necessary for a Christian minister to defend his character and to explain his conduct. Usually it is better for him to suffer in silence and to await the vindication which God will give in eternity if not in time. Paul felt that the charge of insincerity had been circulated so widely in the church at Corinth that it was necessary to begin his letter by removing certain misgivings and suspicions which he believed to be in the minds of his readers.

He had been charged with fickleness and double-dealing. This charge was based on three alleged grounds. First of all, he was approaching Corinth by a route different from that which he had promised to take. Secondly, after assuring the Corinthians of a speedy visit, he had long delayed his coming. Thirdly, he was now advising leniency toward the very man upon whose punishment he had insisted with such force.

These were not very serious charges, but they were made the grounds for casting aspersions upon the honesty and integrity of the apostle. There is something humiliating in the very fact that a man like Paul should ever be called upon to defend his character. However, human nature is such that even today in Christian communities false motives are imputed and suspicions are aroused so that the most sensitive and unselfish souls are compelled to speak in their own defense.

Paul begins with a positive and emphatic affirmation of his absolute and complete sincerity. He declares this to be a real ground for boasting. His conscience bears witness to the fact that his conduct has been characterized by "a holiness separated from all uncleanness of the world, and an uprightness which if examined by the most brilliant light of the sun will show no defects." He has never relied upon worldly cleverness, but always upon the grace of God. His purity of purpose and the crystal transparency of his conduct have been manifested everywhere, and never more clearly than in his dealings with the Corinthian church. (V. 12.)

This affirmation is closely linked with the thanksgiving with which the letter opens, where he says in effect that he well may expect his readers to pray for his safety, since his conduct has ever been such as to merit their confidence and love. It is also vitally related to the paragraphs which follow, for it states the theme or forms the summary of Paul's entire reply to the three charges, with which he proceeds to deal.

First of all, however, he makes his claim of sincerity more definite by referring to his letters. These seem to have contained the statements upon which the charge of duplicity was based. Paul insists that the meaning of his written words has always been obvious and plain. He has never tried to deceive. No one has been expected to read between the lines. He has said what he meant and has meant what he said. The Corinthians have read what was written and have recognized it as true. Paul hopes they ever will do the same. Indeed, they have always trusted Paul, at least most of them have, and have acknowledged that they have real reason for glorying in him as their spiritual father. Similarly he expects to be proud of them, in the day when Christ returns.

The mention of that day, on which all thoughts will be revealed, confirms Paul's claim of sincerity. He has no fear of what will then be disclosed as to his motives and conduct. This passage greatly strengthens the introduction to his defense. (Vs. 13-14.)

As to the change of plan, Paul admits that he had intended to visit Corinth by a different route. He had hoped to come by the short course across the sea and then to journey northward to Macedonia; he had planned to return again to Corinth from Macedonia, and then to be helped forward by his Corinthian friends as he started for Judea. This plan had been formed "in this confidence" of mutual trust and esteem which he has just described. He did not suppose that his plans would be regarded as a ground for suspecting his motives or traducing his character. "In wishing to come by the longer route," writes the apostle, "did I show levity?" He refers to that lightness of character which permits a man to make a promise he has no intention of fulfilling. "Or are my purposes usually like those of a man of the world who is animated by fleshly motives, unstable, insincere? Are they to be interpreted at the same time as meaning both 'Yes, yes' and 'No, no'?" Of the truth of such suspicions and of

false charges of insincerity, Paul makes a solemn denial.
"As God is faithful, our word toward you is not yea and
nay." Neither his proposed plans nor the gospel he
preached was vacillating, contradictory, unreliable. His
gospel message centered in the Son of God, Jesus Christ.
Surely the Christ who had been preached by Paul and
his companions is not a Christ of uncertainty or contra-
dictions. He is not a waverer between yes and no, but
in him is ever found a divine "Yes"; for all the promises
made by God in the Old Testament find in Christ their
confirmation, their fulfillment, their guarantee. "In him
is yea." Wherefore also through him those who believe
in him express their "Amen." They attest God's truthfulness and faithfulness. They glorify God. They declare
that they have found in personal experience all that was
contained in God's precious promises. To the question,
"Will God's promises be fulfilled?" Christ is the Answer,
the incarnate "Yes," the everlasting "Yea." So through
him comes, from the believers who have experienced this
fulfillment, the glad "Amen," "It is so." This experience of theirs had been brought to pass through Paul.
Could it be then that he was guilty of such weakness and
instability as have been imputed to him?

Thus it appears that Paul argues from the character of
his preaching to the quality of his conduct. Such a message as his could not have come from a man who was
fickle and unreliable in his own resolves and promises.

This argument is not in every case conclusive. A man's
preaching is not always an index to his life. However,
when, as in the case of Paul, a man's whole soul is ab-
sorbed in declaring the faithfulness of God, it is incredible
that he should himself be faithless and false; and, furthermore, when his message centers in the fulfillment of God's
promises, he is not likely to be untrue to his own. (Vs.
15-20.)

Paul further argues, however, that his character, which
has been called in question and traduced, is a divine crea-

tion. It cannot be untrue and insincere, for it is a product of the grace of the ever-faithful God. What he claims for himself, as this striking defense of his personal sincerity is brought to a close, he attributes likewise to his readers and to all the followers of Christ.

Whatever stability of character we possess is attributed to God. It is he who establishes us in a steadfast relation to Christ. It is he who makes us partakers of the very life of his Anointed. He has indeed "anointed us." In earlier days prophets and priests and kings were anointed with oil as a symbol of the influence of God's Spirit, by which they were to be equipped for their tasks. So, in reality, God anoints us for our service. The gracious influences of his Spirit prepare us for our work and consecrate us to the service of Christ.

By the same Spirit we are "also sealed." Now a seal was a sign of ownership, a warrant of safety, an impress of likeness. So, the abiding presence of the Spirit of God is a sign that we belong to God. It is further an assurance of our salvation. It is even now imprinting upon us some likeness to our God.

Furthermore, the Spirit dwelling in our hearts is an earnest of the glory which yet awaits us. An earnest was not only a pledge; it was a partial payment. It was a first installment of the thing which had been promised. So the Holy Spirit is for us an earnest of the life eternal, which in all its fullness we are to enjoy. As an earnest was the same in kind as the promised possession, we know that the essence and glory of the blessedness which awaits us must be spiritual; we are to be transformed into the likeness of our Lord.

2. The Delayed Visit   Chs. 1:23 to 2:4

23 But I call God for a witness upon my soul, that to spare you I forbare to come unto Corinth. 24 Not that we have lordship over your faith, but are helpers of your

joy: for in faith ye stand fast.   1 But I determined this for
myself, that I would not come again to you with sorrow.
2 For if I make you sorry, who then is he that maketh me
glad but he that is made sorry by me?   3 And I wrote this
very thing, lest, when I came, I should have sorrow from
them of whom I ought to rejoice; having confidence in you
all, that my joy is the joy of you all.   4 For out of much
affliction and anguish of heart I wrote unto you with many
tears; not that ye should be made sorry, but that ye might
know the love which I have more abundantly unto you.

Paul had changed his plan.   This had involved a delay
in his proposed visit to Corinth.   Instead of coming by
the short direct route westward across the sea, he was
approaching by way of Troas and Philippi.   In the previous paragraph he declared that his change of plan was
not due to fickleness or levity.   He now explains the reason for his altered purpose and his consequent delay.   It
was not due to caprice or cowardice or personal con-
venience but was wholly out of consideration for the Corinthian church.

The solemnity of his language shows how deeply he
felt the charge that he had been insincere.   He calls God
to witness the truth of his statement.   He says that his
soul shall answer for anything false he may utter.   He then
declares that it was to spare the members of the church
that he delayed his visit to Corinth.   They were not ready
for his return.   His coming would have caused them pain.
He must have exercised severe discipline.   He wished to
give them time to repent.

At once, however, the thought comes to Paul that this
statement may be misinterpreted.   The desire to spare
implies the power to punish, and the claim of this power
may imply a claim to complete lordship and control.   So
to avoid giving offense he denies any desire to dictate or
to domineer.

"Not that we have lordship over your faith."   Do not
think we presume to do this.   Faith must be free.   One

cannot make an unconvinced man believe. The most one can do is to make him say that he believes. In the matter of faith all that Christian ministers can do is to instruct, to encourage, and to guide. They can be fellow workers with believers, and can lead them as helpers of their joy. This was what Paul wished to do. He had no thought of controlling faith, for in the sphere of faith the Corinthians stood steadfast.

Because he wished to increase their happiness and not to cause them sorrow, he had refrained from visiting them at the time when his coming would have been painful both to him and to them. "But I determined this for myself," he writes, "that I would not come again to you with sorrow." The words seem to indicate that he had paid to Corinth a visit in sorrow since that happier visit which had resulted in the founding of the Corinthian church. The later distressing experience he was unwilling to repeat. He did not wish to cause the Corinthians sorrow, for they, his dear friends in Christ, were the very persons whom he wished might welcome him with joy, and impart to him gladness and cheer. He could not think of causing such persons pain and grief. He thought it better to stay away until he could come to them in joy. This is the very thing he had said to them in a previous letter which he had written instead of coming to Corinth, namely, that to spare them he had given up the idea of coming, lest by coming he might be pained by those in whom he ought to find gladness. For he had confidence in the perfect sympathy between himself and them, and he knew their delight and joy was in giving him joy.

He had written that previous letter in intense "affliction and anguish of heart." He had shed many tears as he wrote it. Yet he had not written to wound them, but that, in showing his anxious desire for their good, he might make them see how his love abounded toward them.

The letter to which Paul refers can hardly be his first epistle to the Corinthians. Of that letter only brief frag-

ments reveal such deep emotion and mental distress as he
here describes. It is therefore quite probable that since
his first stay in Corinth, Paul not only had paid a brief,
painful visit to that city, but also had written a severe
letter of stern rebuke to the Corinthian church. That letter has caused him real anguish of soul. Yet such sorrow
could only be felt by one who cherished for his readers
the most tender sympathy and the most ardent love.

In such passages as this the very heart of the apostle
is revealed. Here is the ideal for every minister of Christ.
No perfunctory performance of duty, no mere intellectual
presentation of truth, can affect the lives and touch the
consciences of men. Only one who feels sorrow and joy,
who sheds tears and is torn by passion, who trusts others
and suffers in sympathy, can expect to be of abiding influence in the service of Christ and his church.

3. THE PENITENT OFFENDER   Ch. 2:5-11

*5 But if any hath caused sorrow, he hath caused sorrow,
not to me, but in part (that I press not too heavily) to you
all. 6 Sufficient to such a one is this punishment which
was* inflicted *by the many; 7 so that contrariwise ye should
rather forgive him and comfort him, lest by any means
such a one should be swallowed up with his overmuch sorrow. 8 Wherefore I beseech you to confirm your love
toward him. 9 For to this end also did I write, that I
might know the proof of you, whether ye are obedient in
all things. 10 But to whom ye forgive anything, I* forgive
*also: for what I also have forgiven, if I have forgiven any-
thing, for your sakes* have I forgiven it *in the presence of
Christ; 11 that no advantage may be gained over us by
Satan: for we are not ignorant of his devices.*

It is easy to play the Pharisee, to be critical and cen-
sorious, cruel and unforgiving. Even Christians are apt
to thank God that they are "not as the rest of men." Of
course, one should not countenance evil and encourage

sin. However, when the sinner has repented and turned from his evil way, then obedience to the law of Christ demands that such a one should be restored in a spirit of meekness, and that his fellow Christians should consider their own weakness and proneness to fall when tempted.

This law of love Paul found the Corinthians unwilling to obey. In fact, when he urged the punishment of an offender, and then asked them to forgive him when penitent, they were ready to accuse the apostle of fickleness and vacillation and duplicity.

Therefore, when he has explained his sincerity in delaying his visit to Corinth and in changing his route of travel, Paul turns to consider the case of this penitent offender. He insists that the man should be forgiven lest he be driven to despair.

Just who this offender was no one can now determine. Many feel that he was the gross sinner upon whose severe discipline the apostle had insisted in the fifth chapter of his first epistle to the Corinthians. Others consider that the language here used can hardly refer to so grievous an offense, and they suppose that the reference is to some insult or affront from which the apostle himself suffered when on his second visit to Corinth, of which we have no detailed record.

Accordingly, it is impossible to know exactly what penalty had been inflicted. It may have been the dread sentence pronounced by Paul in his first epistle, or some milder form of discipline administered to one who had insulted the apostle and defied his authority.

The sorrow, Paul declared, had not been caused so much to himself as to the church, or at least to part of the church. The punishment which had been inflicted by the majority of the members was quite sufficient. The man should be pardoned and comforted lest he be overwhelmed by remorse. The Corinthians should show him their love. This advice does not contradict Paul's previous letter. He wrote urging discipline to test the obedi-

ence of the church.   The penalty they inflicted showed
their loyalty.   Their forgiveness would surely meet his
approval as of one who acted with Christ as a witness.
The offender should be restored lest by driving him to despair, his fellow Christians allow Satan to capture him from
them.   Of the evil designs of the adversary they were not
ignorant.

Thus, while it is impossible to determine beyond question either the particular offense or its punishment, the
practical principles involved in this passage are plain and
important.   Among these abiding principles the following
may be named: (*a*) No church should fail to discipline
its offending members.   (*b*) This discipline should not be
administered by the decision of any one man in the church,
but by the will of the majority of the members.   (*c*) The
one supreme purpose of such discipline should be the reformation and reclamation of the offender.   (*d*) When the
offender is penitent he should receive forgiveness and be
treated with affection.   (*e*) Severity and lack of sympathy
may drive the offender to desperation and again place him
under the power of Satan.

D. THE NATURE OF PAUL'S MINISTRY
Chs. 2:12 to 6:10

1. TRIUMPHANT   Ch. 2:12-17

*12 Now when I came to Troas for the gospel of Christ,
and when a door was opened unto me in the Lord, 13 I
had no relief for my spirit, because I found not Titus my
brother: but taking my leave of them, I went forth into
Macedonia.*

*14 But thanks be unto God, who always leadeth us in
triumph in Christ, and maketh manifest through us the
savor of his knowledge in every place.   15 For we are a
sweet savor of Christ unto God, in them that are saved, and
in them that perish;   16 to the one a savor from death
unto death; to the other a savor from life unto life.   And*

*who is sufficient for these things?   17 For we are not as
the many, corrupting the word of God: but as of sincerity,
but as of God, in the sight of God, speak we in Christ.*

Paul has just explained his course of action. He has
defended himself against the charge of fickleness. He had
changed his plan and instead of a visit had sent the Corinthians a letter by the hand of Titus. His wisdom in
thus delaying his visit was evident from the action of the
church in disciplining the offending member. He now
recalls how anxiously he had awaited the news of their
action and of their attitude toward him. Titus had
planned to meet Paul at Troas with tidings from Corinth.
On reaching Troas, and finding that Titus had not arrived, Paul refused a great opportunity for evangelistic
work and pressed on to Macedonia, so eager was he to
receive word from the Corinthian church. "Now when I
came to Troas," he writes, "for the gospel of Christ," i.e.,
on his missionary journey, "and when a door was opened
unto me in the Lord," i.e., an unusual opportunity of
Christian service, "I had no relief for my spirit, because
I found not Titus my brother." "Therefore," he declares,
"I bade good-by to my friends and converts and crossed
over to Macedonia."

Here in Macedonia, possibly at Philippi, he at last met
Titus with the news for which he longed. So favorable
was the word, such relief it brought to the heart of Paul,
that he does not pause to record or to describe it. He
breaks off in a doxology. He praises God for the divine
deliverance and success which always attend his work, and
he begins a long digression in which he describes the character of his ministry. Indeed he does not resume his
reference to Titus and his message until the fifth verse of
the seventh chapter.

The first characteristic, then, of Paul's ministry is its
continual triumph; so at least he feels as he rises suddenly
out of his anguish of suspense and learns how fully the

Corinthians have obeyed him and how truly they trust him.

The whole paragraph is phrased in figures borrowed from the scene of triumph in which a victorious general swept through the streets of imperial Rome. In pomp and glory, crowned with laurel, mounted on his chariot, preceded by the senate, magistrates, musicians, the spoils, and the captives in chains, the proud conqueror ascended the Capitoline Hill, leading his exultant hosts. Clouds of incense filled the air with perfume. The miserable captives turned aside to die, while the praise of the victor was shouted by the multitudes amid a tumult of applause.

In such terms Paul describes his experience. The dominant note is that of triumph. However, God is the Victor. He is making the victorious progress. Paul is like one who is given a part in this triumphal pageant. The thought is not either that Paul is made a victor or that he is exhibited as a captive, but that God associates him in the divine triumph of his redeeming work.

Paul's joyful experience in being delivered from his anxiety for the Corinthians is only an example of a ministry which is ever glorious in its triumph. His whole experience is said to be "in Christ." This is the sphere in which Paul's inner life ever moved.

Through Paul the knowledge of God is being spread abroad. This knowledge is like sweet perfume; it rises like the smoke of the incense in the midst of which marched the conqueror's train. Yet Paul is not merely the medium by which the perfume is being diffused; he is himself the "sweet savor of Christ"; for Christ lives in the apostle even as the apostle lives in Christ, and through Paul is being breathed the saving knowledge of God.

There are, however, two classes of men among whom this perfume circulates, those on the way to salvation and those on the way to perdition; as in a triumphal procession there were the conqueror and his troops, and the conquered captives, all breathing the perfume of the same incense. To the victors the fragrance was a symbol of present gladness and of future safety; to the captives it was a token of defeat and condemnation and a premonition of approaching death. Such are the different effects of the gospel. It works either life or death. The rejected blessing only deepens the condemnation and makes more sure the doom. The intended effect of the gospel is life. Its accidental effect through sin and blindness may be death.

The solemnity of the situation forces from the apostle the cry, "Who is sufficient for these things?" Who possesses the love, the wisdom, the humility, the earnestness for a calling, the issues of which are eternal life or death? Who can so preach as to produce the redemptive effects of the gospel?

One might imagine that Paul would reply in despair, "No one is sufficient." Quite on the contrary, with startling assurance, he declares himself to be sufficient for such a task. Yet his sufficiency is not of himself. As far as he is concerned the one condition which he fulfills is that of downright honesty. He contrasts himself with other teachers. They indeed are not sufficient for such a task. They are guilty of "corrupting the word of God," that is, they are "making merchandise" of it. They are using the gospel for their own selfish advantage. They are adulterating the truth; like dishonest merchants they are mixing the wine with water; they are falsifying the thing which they sell. In striking contrast, the apostle again declares his own absolute "sincerity." His motives are pure, his methods honorable. God is the Source of his message. He speaks "in the sight of God," as the witness of his ministry. He speaks also as one who finds "in Christ" his whole sphere of action. Such a minister is sufficient for the solemn task of proclaiming the gospel of grace. Such a ministry will ever be triumphant.

2. ACCREDITED   Ch. 3:1-3

*1 Are we beginning again to commend ourselves? or
need we, as do some, epistles of commendation to you or
from you?   2 Ye are our epistle, written in our hearts,
known and read of all men;   3 being made manifest that
ye are an epistle of Christ, ministered by us, written not
with ink, but with the Spirit of the living God; not in tables
of stone, but in tables* that are *hearts of flesh.*

The very best credentials for a Christian minister are
to be found in the lives and characters of his people.
These prove the quality of his work. At least so Paul
assumes as he writes to his Christian converts at Corinth.

He has just defended his own sincerity and has claimed
to be competent to preach a gospel which involves the
issues of life and death. This may have sounded like
self-praise, and one of the charges preferred by his enemies had evidently been that of self-assertion and pride.
The charge was evidently based, in part at least, upon the
tone of authority which the apostle had been compelled
to assume in his previous epistle. However that may
have been, he assures his readers that he is not "beginning again to commend" himself. There is no necessity
of that. Nor does he, like some people, need letters of
commendation either to or from the Corinthians. He is
here giving a severe side blow to his enemies, certain false
teachers, who seem to have come to Corinth with com-
mendatory letters from Jerusalem. Paul needs no such
certificates. He shows why. The Corinthians are his
"epistle." He remembers with joyful heart how he
brought them to Christ; all men can know and read the
character of his apostolic work as they become acquainted
with these Corinthian converts. All will recognize these
Christians as a letter which Christ has composed and
published, using Paul as his instrument.

This letter has been written, "not in ink," which might
fade, but by the changeless "Spirit of the living God."

It was not written on "tables of stone," as was the law of Moses, but on living tablets of sensitive human hearts. It would have been more natural for the apostle to say, "Not on parchment or on paper, but on human hearts." However, he already has in mind the contrast between the glory of the law and the glory of the gospel which will occupy the rest of the chapter. So here he refers to the tables of stone rather than to ordinary materials for writing.

He intimates that this living "epistle of Christ," which constitutes his credentials, is superior not only to any formal letters of recommendation which may have been brought by his enemies, but even, in some respects, to the tables of Sinai. The latter were indeed "written . . . with the Spirit of the living God," but they were in themselves inert, and were powerless to touch the hearts of men; the living epistle by which Paul was accredited was able to bear witness not only to a human worker but to a divine Redeemer.

In connection with this paragraph it is almost inevitable to recall the fact that so many letters of commendation are meaningless and misleading and insincere. It is the duty of every Christian to remember that his life should be an epistle "known and read of all men," so sincere, so true, so honest, that in it all men will see the handiwork, the touch, the impress of the Spirit of the living God, witnessing to the glory and grace of Christ.

3. GLORIOUS   Ch. 3:4-18

4 And such confidence have we through Christ to God-ward: 5 not that we are sufficient of ourselves, to account anything as from ourselves; but our sufficiency is from God; 6 who also made us sufficient as ministers of a new covenant; not of the letter, but of the spirit: for the letter killeth, but the spirit giveth life. 7 But if the ministration of death, written, and engraven on stones, came with glory, so that the children of Israel could not look stedfastly upon

the face of Moses for the glory of his face; which glory
*was passing away: 8 how shall not rather the ministration
of the spirit be with glory?   9 For if the ministration of
condemnation hath glory, much rather doth the ministration of righteousness exceed in glory.   10 For verily that
which hath been made glorious hath not been made glorious in this respect, by reason of the glory that surpasseth.
11 For if that which passeth away* was *with glory, much
more that which remaineth* is *in glory.*

*12 Having therefore such a hope, we use great boldness
of speech, 13 and* are *not as Moses,* who *put a veil upon
his face, that the children of Israel should not look stedfastly on the end of that which was passing away: 14 but
their minds were hardened: for until this very day at the
reading of the old covenant the same veil remaineth, it not
being revealed* to them *that it is done away in Christ.   15
But unto this day, whensoever Moses is read, a veil lieth
upon their heart.   16 But whensoever it shall turn to the
Lord, the veil is taken away.   17 Now the Lord is the
Spirit: and where the Spirit of the Lord is,* there *is liberty.
18 But we all, with unveiled face beholding as in a mirror
the glory of the Lord, are transformed into the same image
from glory to glory, even as from the Lord the Spirit.*

Paul is describing his ministry.   He has declared it to
be triumphant and fully accredited.   He now exhibits its
glory.   He does this by comparing the gospel of Christ
with the law of Moses.   The latter was glorious, but the
gospel has a glory which surpasses that of the law.

This is no chance or casual comparison.   It is connected with the paragraphs which precede and relate to
the purpose of this entire section of the epistle.   In these
first seven chapters Paul is declaring his principles of action.   He is doing so to prepare the Corinthians for his
approaching visit.   He must remove from their minds
the suspicions inspired by his enemies.   These false teachers had come from Jerusalem with letters of commendation.   They were insisting that Christians must keep the
ceremonial law imposed by Moses, and they denounced

Paul as a false apostle because he denied the necessity of
these legal observances.

These false teachers were ever in mind. Thus, in declaring the triumphant nature of his ministry, he stated
that he was "not as the many, corrupting the word of
God," adding impure ingredients, adulterating the pure
gospel with ingredients from the law, as was being done
by his enemies. Also, when declaring that the Corinthians
constituted his letter of commendation to the world, he
stated that "some" needed formal certificates and written
credentials. He did not; his enemies did.

When he is reaching the very heart of his statement of
the splendor of his Christian apostleship, he uses, by way
of illustration, the story of the giving of the law to Moses
and the shining and the veiling of his face. One feature
of the familiar story has been commonly misunderstood
by Christians for the past three hundred years. Due to
the misplacement of one word in the Authorized Version
it frequently has been believed that Moses veiled his face
so that he could speak with the people, who were afraid
of its brightness. The fact is that he veiled his face after
speaking to the people, so that they might not see the
glory fade from his countenance. The Authorized Version reads, *"Till* Moses had done speaking with them, he
put a veil on his face." It should read, *"When* Moses
had done speaking with them, he put a veil on his face"
(Ex. 34:33 RV).

The story is simply this. Moses went up on to the
mount to receive from the Lord the tables of the law. In
the divine presence his face shone with a reflected light.
When he came down from the mountain the people saw
the glory on his countenance and were afraid. But he
called to them and they came near. And when he had
done speaking with them he put a veil on his face that
they might not see the glory fade away. When he turned
back to speak with the Lord he removed the veil and his
face again began to shine with a new light. This story is

continually in Paul's mind as he sets forth the majestic character of his gospel ministry. He rebukes his enemies who boasted their allegiance to the law, and he makes plain the surpassing splendor of his Christian apostleship.

He begins by saying that his confidence in the Corinthian church as a sufficient credential of his apostolic authority is no false fancy. It comes through Christ and it looks to God as its source. (V. 4.)

He has not been guilty of self-praise when claiming to be sufficient for the solemn task of proclaiming the gospel. (Ch. 2:17.) He does not count himself even qualified to estimate his services as the author of the work done at Corinth. The existence of the Corinthian church indicates that he must have been competent, but all his sufficiency has come from God. (Ch. 3:5.)

From that divine Source has come the necessary ability and grace to serve as the minister of a new covenant, a new dispensation. The word "ministers" here used, as always in the New Testament, is not an official title. It means "servants." Paul and his companions had been given the privilege of administering, of proclaiming, a new covenant. This is described as being one which does not consist of a written code, but has as its essence the work of the divine Spirit. It is vastly superior to the covenant administered by Moses. That covenant imposed death for disobedience to its solemn demands; the gospel brings men into vital contact with the life-giving Spirit.

Paul's contrast between "the letter" and "the spirit" is one of the most commonly abused phrases in the New Testament. It is usually supposed to contrast the literal with the spiritual meaning of any text or teaching. The real contrast is between the law of Moses, which consists of a written code, and the gospel of Christ, which speaks of the transforming power of the divine Spirit. This is the real meaning of the phrase, "The letter killeth, but the spirit giveth life" (v. 6).

The law of Moses was indeed glorious. Even though

its solemn sanctions made it a "ministration of death," even though it was a thing "written, and engraven on stones," nevertheless it must have been glorious if, at its inauguration, the face of the lawgiver shone with such dazzling brightness that the Children of Israel could not look upon it.

Yet that brightness soon faded. Its transient splendor is a fit symbol of the glory of the law, which has grown dim in comparison with the surpassing splendor of the gospel, which is "a dispensation of God." If the mission of Moses was glorious, much more is the ministry of Paul. For if the dispensation which brings the sentence of death came with glory, much more glorious must be that dispensation which offers righteousness as a free gift to men. (Vs. 7-9.) The former may be regarded in comparison as lacking real glory because its glory fades and disappears before the overwhelming glory of the latter. For while that which is transient does have something of glory, that which abides is truly arrayed in far greater glory. (Vs. 10-11.)

"As ministers of Christ we are supported by the confident expectation that the glory of the gospel will never fade," says Paul, speaking for the Christian ministers. "Therefore we preach with great confidence and openness and courage. In contrast with some others, we have nothing to conceal. We are not like Moses. He used to put a veil over his face, so that the Children of Israel should not gaze at the dying rays of the glory which the presence of the Lord had imparted to his countenance. The fading of that glory was a symbol of the transitory character of the Mosaic dispensation. The Children of Israel, however, instead of seeing what that fading splendor meant, have grown dull in their spiritual perception, for, to this very day, when the Old Testament is read, from which they might learn this very lesson, a veil of ignorant unbelief hangs over their hearts. They do not perceive the transitory character of the Mosaic law, and do not see that its glory fades in the presence of Christ. Yes, down to this very day, whenever the law of Moses is read in their synagogues the same veil of blindness rests upon their hearts. However, just as Moses removed the veil from his face when he returned to the presence of the Lord, so when any one of them turns to the Lord the veil is removed from his heart and he sees that the glory of the law has faded before the surpassing glory of the gospel." (Vs. 12-16.)

"Now the Lord to whom such a one turns is the Spirit of Christ; and where the Spirit of Christ is, there is freedom from the bondage of the Mosaic law. It is not a freedom which is license to disregard law, but a liberty to do the very thing the law demands. The law placed restriction on outward conduct; the Spirit of Christ transforms the inner life. To turn from the law to Christ is, therefore, to turn from a code which enslaves by its precepts and penalties to a Spirit who gives liberty and life. Instead of the bondage of fear, the believer enjoys the free service of love; instead of a bondage to sin due to weakness, there comes the liberty of a new power and a divinely given life." (V. 17.)

"So all of us who believe in Christ are like Moses, when the veil was taken from his face, and when he gazed upon the glory of the Lord. The veil has been taken from our hearts. In the face of Christ, as in a mirror, we see the glory of the Lord. We gaze upon him in faith and in love. Before the brightness of his face, the fading glory of our old life of self-righteousness and self-dependence, of legalism and ritualism, of weakness and bondage and failure, grows dim and disappears. Instead of reflecting the glory of the Lord merely in our faces, as Moses did, we experience an inner transformation of character. We are changed into the very likeness of Christ, not instantly, but gradually from one degree of glory to another. This transformation is not by the power of human resolution, or by an effort at imitation, but by the gracious influence of the Lord, by the presence and indwelling of the Spirit of Christ." (V. 18.)

Paul thus demonstrates the superiority of the grace of God in Christ to all human methods of salvation, and to all other proposals for securing peace and holiness and life. In at least three particulars, he shows the dispensation of the gospel to be more glorious than that of the law. First, the principle is that of an indwelling Spirit rather than that of enforced obedience to an external code. Second, the permanence of the gospel is contrasted with all the changing and vanishing systems of the world's beliefs and religions. Even Judaism with all its actual glory, with its divine appointments and ordinances, was a system of types and symbols and shadows. It was temporary, preparatory. Its glory faded when the fulfillment had come, when the reality appeared. That glory was "done away in Christ." Third, the power revealed in the gospel is not that of renewed human effort and resolution, which results in an outward imitation, a mere temporary reflection of glory, but that of the Lord himself, who, dwelling within the heart, is ready to transform into the likeness of his Son all those who put their trust in him.

Surely if the mission of Moses, the greatest of all lawgivers, was glorious, much more glorious is the ministry of Paul, and of all true messengers of the gospel of Christ.

4. HONEST   Ch. 4:1-6

1 Therefore seeing we have this ministry, even as we obtained mercy, we faint not: 2 but we have renounced the hidden things of shame, not walking in craftiness, nor handling the word of God deceitfully; but by the manifestation of the truth commending ourselves to every man's conscience in the sight of God. 3 And even if our gospel is veiled, it is veiled in them that perish: 4 in whom the god of this world hath blinded the minds of the unbelieving, that the light of the gospel of the glory of Christ, who is the image of God, should not dawn upon them. *5 For we preach not ourselves, but Christ Jesus as Lord, and ourselves as your servants for Jesus' sake. 6 Seeing it is God, that said, Light shall shine out of darkness, who shined in our hearts, to give the light of the knowledge of the glory of God in the face of Jesus Christ.*

It is hard to believe that a man like Paul could have been accused of dishonesty, of duplicity, and of deceit. Yet such was the case. Human nature is ever prone to suspicion, to envy, and to slander. Even such a saint could not escape, and a large part of this epistle is an endeavor on the part of the apostle to establish his sincerity, his truthfulness, and his honesty of purpose.

This paragraph, in which such endeavor is most obvious, is inseparably connected with that which precedes and which sets forth the glory of Paul's ministry and of the gospel. Just because the gospel is so glorious, Paul has no temptation to falsify, to conceal, or to deceive. Just because it is so glorious he is encouraged to continue its proclamation with openness and frankness and boldness.

" 'Therefore seeing we have this ministry,' this glorious service of proclaiming the gospel," Paul says, "and remembering the mercy God has shown in appointing us to such a task and in making us sufficient for its demands, 'we faint not,' we never lose heart, we feel no timidity, or shame, and are not compelled to take refuge in silence and inactivity. 'We have renounced the hidden things of shame,' the underhand practices of false teachers; indeed we have never followed any course which could be regarded as shameful or unscrupulous. Nor have we laid ourselves open to the charge of adulterating the gospel message, and of handling it deceitfully." Such charges may be brought against others; Paul insists they cannot be brought against him. On the contrary, he has proclaimed the truth openly and honestly, and has thereby commended himself to every man's conscience. He has spoken as one whose work is "in the sight of God," and he wishes to be judged by God.

It is true that the gospel he declares so openly is hidden from some. Its meaning is not understood. Just as a veil concealed from the Children of Israel the light with which the face of Moses was shining, so unbelief blinds some men, and they fail to see the glory which streams from the face of Christ. Paul describes them as perishing; for Satan has blinded their minds. As a result, the morning glow, the bursting dawn of the gospel, does not reach them. They fail to behold the light of good tidings concerning the glory of Christ, who is himself "the image of God," the Embodiment of all divine perfection.

Paul has no need of subterfuge or deceit. No true preacher has. He is not seeking to secure praise or power for himself. His whole endeavor is to make men submit themselves to Christ as their Lord and Master. "For we preach not ourselves, but Christ Jesus as Lord, and ourselves as your servants for Jesus' sake."

Here Paul uses the name "Jesus," the human title, the word indicating the voluntary humility of our Lord. "We are your bondservants, for the sake of him, and in the service of him, who for our sakes took the form of a bondservant."

"We have no glory of our own to proclaim," says Paul. "We have no personal ends to gain. The knowledge and the message we possess have come from God. As at the creation he called light into being by his divine word, 'Light shall shine out of darkness,' so he has caused spiritual light, even the knowledge of his saving grace in Christ, to spring up in our hearts. Nor has this been that we might keep and enjoy it for ourselves, but that we might convey to others this knowledge of God, this heavenly light which shines with undimmed splendor in the countenance of the Lord."

Thus, as in the preceding paragraph, Paul sets forth the glory of the gospel, the pitiful state of those who refuse to accept its light, and its source in the grace of God.   Furthermore, he shows the honesty and courage, the glorious privilege and the unselfish service, of every true minister of Christ.

5. SUFFERING   Ch. 4:7-18

7 But we have this treasure in earthen vessels, that the exceeding greatness of the power may be of God, and not from ourselves;   8 we are pressed on every side, yet not straitened; perplexed, yet not unto despair;   9 pursued, yet not forsaken; smitten down, yet not destroyed;   10 always bearing about in the body the dying of Jesus, that the life also of Jesus may be manifested in our body. 11 For we who live are always delivered unto death for Jesus' sake, that the life also of Jesus may be manifested in our mortal flesh.   12 So then death worketh in us, but life in you.   13 But having the same spirit of faith, according to that which is written, I believed, and therefore did I speak; we also believe, and therefore also we speak;   14 knowing that he that raised up the Lord Jesus shall raise up us also with Jesus, and shall present us with you.   15 For all things are for your sakes, that the grace, being multiplied through the many, may cause the thanksgiving to abound unto the glory of God.

16 Wherefore we faint not; but though our outward man is decaying, yet our inward man is renewed day by day. 17 For our light affliction, which is for the moment, worketh for us more and more exceedingly an eternal weight of glory;   18 while we look not at the things which are seen, but at the things which are not seen: for the things which are seen are temporal; but the things which are not seen are eternal.

Paul has been setting forth the glory of the gospel; he now turns to contrast the sufferings of its ministers.   In these sufferings they are sustained by divine power and by the hope of future glory.   The expression of this hope illumines the picture of their sufferings, and bursts into a blaze of splendor as this chapter comes to its close and the next chapter opens. First of all, however, Paul dwells upon the divine power which is the more marvelously manifested because of the very frailty of the ministers in whom it is revealed.

"But we have this treasure in earthen vessels" (fragile vases of clay), he declares, this treasure of "the knowledge of the glory of God in the face of Jesus Christ." The reference is probably to the ancient practice among Orientals of storing gold and silver in earthenware jars. It is his weak and suffering body which Paul here compares to an earthen vessel, yet probably not his body alone, but his whole being, with its human infirmities and imperfections. This is "the lamp of frail ware in which the light of Christ's glory shines for the illumination of the world." The very frailty of the minister enhanced the glory of God. It made more evident the fact that only by divine power was the apostle sustained and made the means of saving souls. The treasure has been placed in vessels of mere earth, "that the exceeding greatness of the power may be of God, and not from ourselves" (v. 7).

To contrast his own weakness with the power of God, Paul suddenly changes the figure of speech. He pictures himself as a soldier in the most dire straits, yet ever delivered by divine grace. With a few strokes of the pen he describes the successive stages of a battle. The warrior is surrounded, hard pressed, driven from the field, struck by the enemy's sword, given over to death; yet marvelously rescued by an unseen Friend. "We are hard pressed on every side," says Paul, speaking of Christ's ministers, "yet not hemmed in and driven to surrender; in desperate plight, yet not in despair; perplexed, yet not baffled; pursued by men, yet not deserted by God; struck to the ground, yet never slain; always carrying about in the body the imminent danger of dying at the hands of foes as Jesus died, in order that by continual deliverances of our bodies it may be manifest to the world that Jesus still lives." (V. 10.)

"Yes, every day that we live we are continually being handed over to death, like living victims, for the sake of Jesus. This is in order that in our bodies, which are liable to death, it may be made manifest to all that the living Jesus does deliver and strengthen. Thus all our pains and perils and spiritual pressure, all our sufferings and weakness and pain, are occasion for the risen Lord to manifest to you [Corinthians] his strength and power." (V. 11.)

"Thus by the very distresses which are wearing out our bodies and bringing us to share in the death of Christ, your faith is being strengthened. So while we have the physical suffering and loss, you have the spiritual comfort and gain." (V. 12.)

"But this deliverance to death does not make us sad and silent. We are like the psalmist, who was inspired by his trust in God. He wrote, 'I believed and therefore did I speak.' We have 'the same spirit of faith.' 'We also believe, and therefore also we speak.' We declare with confidence that although our sufferings may end in death, we shall experience a glorious resurrection." (V. 13.)

"We know that God, who 'raised up the Lord Jesus shall raise up us also with Jesus, and shall present us with you.'" Paul does not mean, of course, that the resurrection of Christ is future. He means that, in virtue of the resurrection of Christ and because of our union with Christ, our resurrection is absolutely assured. "Furthermore, on that day of Christ's glorious appearing, God will 'present us with you,' as a bride is presented to her husband. In spite of our being delivered to death our horizon is not bounded by a funeral cortege but by 'the marriage supper of the Lamb.'"

This passage is too frequently forgotten by those who accuse Paul of changing his teaching as to the time of the Advent of Christ. They assert that he assured the Thessalonians, and declared in First Corinthians, that he would live until his Lord returned, and so would never die, but that he wrote to Timothy that the time of his departure was at hand. The fact is that Paul here, as in other passages, unites himself in thought with fellow Christians. When speaking of the Advent he never affirms that it will or will not occur in his lifetime. He indicates that it may. What he does affirm is that, when Christ returns, if he is living, he will be transfigured; if he is dead, he will be raised. This was his attitude of mind, and it has been the blessed hope of the followers of Christ through all the passing years. (V. 14.)

The declaration of such a hope, and the endurance of his present sufferings, Paul declares to be for the sake and for the benefit of his readers. It is in order that the grace bestowed upon them may be shared by an increasing number of believers, and may result in a larger volume of thanksgiving to "the glory of God." (V. 15.)

"No wonder then," the apostle concludes, "that with your interests at heart, and sustained by such divine power, and inspired by such a glorious hope, we faint not; we never lose heart. For, though our physical powers are wasting away, yet our spirits are being continually made fresh and strong. Processes of destruction and renewal are going on at the same time. They are even related. For our present light burden of affliction is working out for us a weight of glory which is of incomparable greatness and is to abide forever. This is true of those of us who are gazing, as toward our goal, not at the things about us which are temporary and fleeting, but at those abiding realities which by us are at present unseen." (Vs. 16-18.)

When Paul speaks of the burden of his affliction and sufferings as "light," he means that they are so only in comparison with the preponderating "weight" of future glory. By "the things which are seen," he refers more particularly to his present sufferings, persecutions, and distress. The "things which are not seen" are immortality, future glory, the vision beatific, and all those blessed certainties which are revealed to us by Christ. The former are temporal, or temporary; not temporal, as belonging to time, but temporary, as being only for a time; they are transitory, fleeting, soon passing away. The "things which are unseen" are permanent, abiding eternal.

Thus Paul reveals the grounds of comfort which sustained him amid the sufferings incident upon his apostolic service. They are the same which can support all the followers of Christ as they suffer for his sake. First, he was assured that his human weakness made more evident the divine power which was working in and through him. Secondly, he was confident that as Christ died and rose again, so, as a follower of Christ, he, too, as he suffered for the sake of Christ, would share the glory of his resurrection. Thirdly, he knew that for one whose gaze was fixed upon Christ, the very sufferings of the present were producing a blessedness which would abide forever.

6. HOPEFUL   Ch. 5:1-10

1 For we know that if the earthly house of our tabernacle be dissolved, we have a building from God, a house not made with hands, eternal, in the heavens. 2 For verily in this we groan, longing to be clothed upon with our habitation which is from heaven: 3 if so be that being clothed we shall not be found naked. 4 For indeed we that are in this tabernacle do groan, being burdened; not for that we would be unclothed, but that we would be clothed upon, that what is mortal may be swallowed up of life. 5 Now he that wrought us for this very thing is God, who gave unto us the earnest of the Spirit. 6 Being therefore always of good courage, and knowing that, whilst we are at home in the body, we are absent from the Lord 7 (for we walk by faith, not by sight); 8 we are of good courage, I say, and are willing rather to be absent from the body, and to be at home with the Lord. 9 Wherefore also we make it our aim, whether at home or absent, to be well-pleasing unto him. 10 For we must all be made manifest before the judgment-seat of Christ; that each one may re-

ceive the things done *in the body, according to what he
hath done, whether* it be *good or bad.*

Paul has been speaking of his sufferings, but also of
his consolations. His ministry is one of suffering but also
of hope. This hope points forward to resurrection and
eternal glory. Even though his frail form is being worn
out by hardship and suffering, even though it may be destroyed by death, his spirit is to be clothed with a body
which is immortal. Someday, for him, death will lose its
sting and the grave its victory.

There is, however, an even brighter aspect of his Christian hope. Paul may never die. He may live until Christ
returns. Then, without dying, his mortal body will be
transformed into the likeness of the glorified body of his
Lord. For, as he wrote in his previous epistle to the
Corinthian Christians, concerning the coming of Christ,
"We all shall not sleep, but we shall all be changed, in a
moment, in the twinkling of an eye." The yearning desire of the apostle was to share this blessed experience, to
escape death and to be gloriously transformed by the
coming of Christ.

Nevertheless, should that desire be denied, should he
experience death, that servant with sable livery would
usher Paul into the radiant presence of his Master, and
he would be "at home with the Lord." Therefore he had
no fear. His one concern was to be well-pleasing to his
Lord, whether he should die or whether he should live
until his return; for he was yet to stand before the judgment seat of Christ.

Of these great truths Paul was absolutely assured, so that
he could say, "We know." This was not the knowledge
of experience, or of human testimony, or of intuition.
It was the knowledge which came to the inspired apostle
by divine revelation. Only thus could one know of resurrection, of transfiguration, and of the glorified body, of
which Paul writes.

"We are sustained in all our sufferings; we are sure that present affliction will issue in eternal glory. For we know that in place of these perishing bodies we are to be given bodies which are immortal. The present body is like a tent in which each one is making his earthly pilgrimage. This will be taken down; but we know that at some time we shall have a better house, a building which God will provide, one that is supernatural, eternal, designed for a heavenly sphere." Such, in substance at least, is the meaning of the apostle. (V. 1.)

Thus he continues: "For truly in this present body we groan and sigh, longing to be clothed with the glorified body which will be ours when Christ comes, since we do not wish to meet him as disembodied spirits." (Vs. 2-3.) "For indeed we that are in these tentlike bodies do groan, feeling oppressed. We do not wish to be separated from our bodies by death. We yearn to have our bodies transformed. Or, to change the figure of speech, we do not wish to be unclothed but 'clothed upon.' We wish to have that which is heavenly placed over that which is earthly. We wish to have what is mortal in the one swallowed up by the immortal life of the other." (V. 4.)

"This consummation is what God has had in view in all that he has wrought for us, in our redemption and new birth, and in all the sanctifying influences of his Spirit. Indeed, the very gift of his Spirit is a pledge of such future glory. He is described in Scripture as the 'earnest of our inheritance.' Thus he who inspired our longing for an immortal body is himself the security that our longing will be fulfilled." (V. 5.)

"Because we have 'the earnest' of the Spirit we are at all times confident of future glory. We are even willing to die, if not privileged to tarry until the Lord comes. We can anticipate that experience with delight, since death will bring us into an even closer and more satisfying relation to Christ than we now enjoy. For we know that 'whilst we are at home in the body, we are absent from the Lord,' not literally speaking, but relatively. For the life of faith is less close and intimate than the life of sight and converse, and it is by means of faith not by means of what we can see that we are held on our way." (V. 7.)

"Cheered by this prospect of entering into the immediate presence of Christ, we are confident and would be well pleased to go into exile from our home in the body and to take up our abode in our home with the Lord." (V. 8.)

"Wherefore, since we are thus as ready to die as to live, we make it our aim to be acceptable to our Lord in the day of his coming." (V. 9.)

"This earnest desire to be acceptable to Christ is but natural when we remember that every one of us must have his whole life and his real character revealed before the judgment seat of Christ, so that each one may receive an award for his actions done in this life, in exact accordance with his conduct, whether it was meritorious or worthless." (V. 10.)

Thus it is evident that Paul's belief in the return of Christ, in the transformation or the resurrection of the body, and in future judgment, had a practical bearing upon his daily life. These great mysteries made his suffering ministry a hopeful ministry.

As to the coming of Christ, he plainly regarded it as an event which might occur in his own lifetime, though he never affirmed that it would. For him, however, it was an inspiring possibility and the center of his Christian hope. He knew that then would occur the transformation of the living and the resurrection of the dead.

As to the state of believers between the time of death and of resurrection, Paul has but few statements to make, but these are of the very deepest significance. What he says as to being "absent from the body" and "at home with the Lord" assures us that this "intermediate state," this disembodied state, is one of blessed and conscious fellowship with Christ. (Phil. 1:20-23; Luke 23:43;

Acts 7:59.)   It is to be preferred to the experience of
this present life; it lacks, however, the full felicity which
is to be enjoyed at the return of Christ, when the immortal spirit will be "clothed upon" with a body of immortal glory.

These blessed realities of the future are largely veiled
in mystery.   Not enough is revealed to satisfy our curi-
osity, but enough to comfort our hearts.   These realities
do not appeal to sentiment alone; they also appeal to the
conscience.   The "vision beatific" and fellowship with the
Lord are no more real than the judgment seat of Christ,
the disclosure of character, and the divine requittal for
conduct.   Life should be lived with these inspiring and
solemn verities more in view.   We should so abide in
Christ "that if he shall be manifested, we may have boldness, and not be ashamed before him at his coming."

7. DEVOTED   Ch. 5:11-17

*11 Knowing therefore the fear of the Lord, we persuade
men, but we are made manifest unto God; and I hope that
we are made manifest also in your consciences.   12 We are
not again commending ourselves unto you, but* speak *as
giving you occasion of glorying on our behalf, that ye may
have wherewith to answer them that glory in appearance,
and not in heart.   13 For whether we are beside ourselves,
it is unto God; or whether we are of sober mind, it is unto
you.   14 For the love of Christ constraineth us; because we
thus judge, that one died for all, therefore all died;   15 and
he died for all, that they that live should no longer live unto
themselves, but unto him who for their sakes died and rose
again.   16 Wherefore we henceforth know no man after the
flesh: even though we have known Christ after the flesh, yet
now we know* him so *no more.   17 Wherefore if any man
is in Christ, he is* a new creature: the old things are passed
away; behold, they are become new.*

Paul is still on the defensive.   He is explaining his
principles of action.   These have been called into question

by his enemies. His conduct seems to have puzzled even some of his friends. Here he reaches the highest point of his defense. Here he discloses the secret of his life. "The love of Christ" is constraining him. His consequent devotion to Christ has made of him a "new creature." Only with this fact in view can his conduct be explained.

He had just been speaking of the immortal hope by which his ministry was sustained. Closely related to this hope was the solemn reality of the "judgment-seat of Christ." With this thought in mind, and knowing by experience the fear of Christ quite as well as the hope of glory, he is attempting to persuade men of his sincerity as a minister of Christ. To God, his aims and motives have already been as clearly revealed as they will be on the Day of Judgment. He hopes that they may be as transparent to his readers and as thoroughly approved by their consciences as they are in the sight of God. (V. 11.)

This may sound like conceit and self-commendation. It is not. He is not indulging in self-praise. His enemies have a way of doing that. He is merely giving his friends an opportunity and a basis for defending him against his opponents and for boasting of their personal knowledge of him in reply to those whose boast is in their external advantages, as they have no moral character of which to be proud. (V. 12.)

Those enemies of the apostle who gloried in their Jewish descent, in their observance of the law, in their reputation for knowledge, had evidently accused Paul not only of insincerity but of insanity. He therefore asserts that if he has seemed to be beside himself it has been due to his zeal for God. If indeed he is sane and sober, he is employing his reason in the service of his friends. In neither case was there ground for imputing to him any selfish motive. (V. 13.)

The explanation of all his activities can be summed up in one illuminating phrase, "The love of Christ constraineth us." This does not mean Paul's love for Christ, but

Christ's love for him. So fully does he realize this love
that he is limited to one course of action. He can turn
aside neither to the right hand nor to the left for any
selfish purpose. He is impelled forward in the ceaseless
service of Christ, constrained by the love of Christ.

This love has been manifested in the death of Christ,
who "died for all." And his death was not only "to their
advantage," it was "in their place." His death was their
death. So really did he die for them that it could be
said, "All died." (V. 14.)

However, this death was in order to make possible a
larger life. As Christ died and rose again, so all who
yield themselves to him die to self and rise to a new and
higher life. This was the very purpose of his death and
his resurrection. He died for them that they should no
longer live for themselves, but should live a new life
devoted to him "who for their sakes died and rose again."
Such has been the experience of Paul; such is the unselfishness of his motives. This answer his readers may give
to all who deny that he is honest or sane or sincere.

His own judgments of men have been greatly influenced
by his Christian experience. Since beginning his new life
in Christ, he has had little regard for mere human distinctions, or natural gifts and abilities, or outward and worldly
advantages. He knows no man "after the flesh." He no
longer regards Christ merely as a man in his human character and relationships. He is concerned with the divine,
risen, glorified Christ. Upon such a Christ his thought
now centers. Such a Christ forms the very sphere in
which he lives. The change in his own experience has
been radical and vital, and this will be true of all those
who are so related to Christ and are resolved to live for
him "who for their sakes died and rose again." "Wherefore if any man is in Christ, he is a new creature: the old
things are passed away," the old standards of judgment,
the old distinctions between men, the old dependence upon
ceremonies and rites, the old purposes and aims, the old

weaknesses and faults, the old pride and conceit, the old
hypocrisies and sins. "Behold, they are become new";
they have given place to generosity and sincerity, righteousness and love.

"The love of Christ," believed, accepted, appreciated,
appropriated, is the supreme motive in the transformation
of human life and character. It may be regarded as the
essence of Christian experience. It is the explanation
which Paul gives of his whole career. "The love of Christ
constraineth us."

It is not the love or the loveliness of a human Christ
which can so transfigure and transform. The knowledge
of the birth and death, of the country, of the conduct, of
the teaching, and of the times of the man Jesus is of real
value and profit to all. However, it is a vital relation to
a divine, glorified, present Christ which makes of one
"a new creature."

Nor must this last term tease and discourage and distress. This new creation defines not only a crisis but a
process. So to accept the Lordship of Christ that one
begins to live in him is to make many familiar things
look old and sordid and shameful. The result will be experiences like those of a new world. However, the picture is ideal as well as real. The actual passing away of
the old, the actual production of the new is a daily process
and experience, a daily task and endeavor. It is ever and
increasingly possible, if in any true sense one lives "in
Christ"; but the full fruition, the complete transformation,
will be known only when in heavenly vision we see him
who sits upon the throne, and hear him say, "Behold, I
make all things new."

8. Reconciling   Ch. 5:18-21

*18 But all things are of God, who reconciled us to him-
self through Christ, and gave unto us the ministry of reconciliation; 19 to wit, that God was in Christ reconciling the*

world unto himself, not reckoning unto them their tres-
passes, and having committed unto us the word of recon-
ciliation.

20 We are ambassadors therefore on behalf of Christ, as
though God were entreating by us: we beseech you *on be-*
half of Christ, be ye reconciled to God. 21 Him who knew
no sin he made to be *sin on our behalf; that we might be-*
come the righteousness of God in him.

The subject is still the sincerity of Paul, which has been impugned by his enemies, and his principles of action, which even his friends have not understood. He has made one supreme, comprehensive explanation, "The love of Christ constraineth us." His knowledge and acceptance of this love have made selfishness and duplicity and dishonesty absolutely impossible. In fact, Paul has been made "a new creature."

He now explains that this spiritual experience and the ministry he is exercising are both from God. There is no place for self-confidence or boasting on the part of a minister of Christ. His message is concerned with an act of divine and gracious reconciliation; and the righteousness he possesses has its source in God alone.

It is true that he has had a new experience. So the apostle is writing. Indeed he is now a new man. He is living in Christ. The sinister motives attributed to him are absolutely inconceivable. However, these changed conditions are no ground for pride. "All things are of God, who reconciled us to himself through Christ, and gave us the ministry of reconciliation."

The new conditions, therefore, were brought about by a divine act of reconciliation and by the commissioning of Paul to make known to others this divine offer of pardon and of peace through Christ. The term "reconciliation" intimates that a state of estrangement had existed between two parties. On the side of man there have been sin and fear and unbelief, separating him from God. On the side of God there have been condemnation of evil and displeasure at disobedience. Through Christ, Paul has had the blessed experience of forgiveness, and of fellowship with God, and has received a call to a new and glorious ministry in the service of Christ.

This "ministry of reconciliation" has one supreme message, namely, that "God was in Christ reconciling the world unto himself." This was being accomplished by canceling for men their debt of guilt, "not reckoning unto them their trespasses," and by committing to the apostles of Christ this message of reconciliation.

Therefore Paul and his companions were ambassadors "on behalf of Christ." Since God himself was speaking through them, they besought their readers to become reconciled to God. On his side God had done all that was necessary for this reconciliation; it was the duty of men to repent of their wrong and to accept the gracious provision he had made.

In the mystery of divine grace, God had made the sinless Christ to take the place of sinful men, that they might receive the righteousness which he in consequence could give.

That Christ "knew no sin" is proved, not merely by the witness of friends and foes but chiefly by the testimony of his own conscience. He never confessed a fault; he never asked for pardon, but he confidently affirmed that no one could convict him of sin. His life was a continual miracle of sinlessness.

However, on our behalf, he was "made to be sin." Not merely did he become a sin offering. In some sense which we cannot fully understand or explain God identified his Son with sin that man might be identified with the righteousness of God.

Christ was not made sinful. He never knew the guilt and degradation of sin, but he did experience its penalty, its dread consequences, its doom. This was with the divine purpose "that we might become the righteousness of God in him."

Therefore, as has been said, "The gospel is not good advice, but good news." It is the announcement to a guilty, hopeless world of a great atoning, redeeming, reconciling act. "Christ died for all." "God was in Christ reconciling the world unto himself." However, the gospel is also good advice, and that of the very highest character. It is a call to all men to accept the gracious provision which God has made: "Be ye reconciled to God."

Paul asserts his dignity as an apostle commissioned to proclaim this good news. Yet this dignity is official and not personal. He is a representative of Christ. He is acting for him.

Furthermore, he exercises his office with great humility. He does not command; he entreats. He does not rebuke; he beseeches. Surely such an ambassador is not to be criticized carelessly or to be slandered rashly; he is a representative of the King. Nor is his message to be lightly received; it is Christ himself who pleads; it is the Father who entreats through the mouth of the apostle. Reconciliation has been made possible by his infinite sacrifice, yet God yearns over man and entreats him to accept the free gift of pardon and peace and righteousness. Could grace be more perfect, could love be more truly divine?

9. APPROVED   Ch. 6:1-10

1 And working together with him *we entreat also that ye receive not the grace of God in vain 2 (for he saith,*
At an acceptable time I hearkened unto thee,
And in a day of salvation did I succor thee:
behold, now is the acceptable time; behold, now is the day of salvation): 3 giving no occasion of stumbling in anything, that our ministration be not blamed; 4 but in everything commending ourselves as ministers of God, in much patience, in afflictions, in necessities, in distresses, 5 in stripes, in imprisonments, in tumults, in labors, in watchings, in fastings; 6 in pureness, in knowledge, in longsuffering, in kindness, in the Holy Spirit, in love un-

feigned, 7 in the word of truth, in the power of God; by the armor of righteousness on the right hand and on the left, 8 by glory and dishonor, by evil report and good report; as deceivers, and yet true; 9 as unknown, and yet well known; as dying, and behold, we live; as chastened, and not killed; 10 as sorrowful, yet always rejoicing; as poor, yet making many rich; as having nothing, and yet possessing all things.

Here Paul's defense of his motives in preaching the gospel and of his principles of action as an apostle is brought to its climax and its close. It is astonishing that one so devoted and so self-sacrificing should have been accused of insincerity and of self-seeking. However, even professed Christians become so blinded by bigotry and self-conceit and fanaticism that, in what they regard as the defense of the truth, they are willing to seize any weapons, including insinuation, slander, and abuse.

In these opening chapters of his epistle, Paul is not answering his enemies directly, as he does in the four closing chapters. He is rather supplying his friends, who form the great majority of the Corinthian church, with grounds on which they may repel the attacks which his enemies are making.

This paragraph is inseparable from the one which precedes. There he has been describing his ministry as one of reconciliation. As an ambassador in behalf of Christ he has been entreating men to be reconciled to God. Here he shows that his conduct and his experiences as an ambassador of God are such as to vindicate fully his claims of genuineness, sincerity, and honesty of purpose.

He describes himself as one who is cooperating with God in the ministry of reconciliation. God has manifested his grace. Paul's part is that of proclaiming this grace; and, more specifically, of entreating the Corinthians that they "receive not the grace of God in vain."

It is hardly an exact use of words for Christians to call themselves "fellow workers with God." At least, there is a popular use of the phrase which is rather superficial and borders on presumption. Christ alone could say, "My Father worketh hitherto, and I work." Only he could make such a claim. In his first epistle (I Cor. 3:9), when Paul spoke of "God's fellow-workers," he meant that he and Apollos were fellow workers who belonged to God and were working for God. There is work which only God can do, and there are forms of work which he does through man. Here Paul means that God, through the gift of his Son, has made reconciliation possible for men, and that Paul is being used to do something which a man can properly do; he is beseeching the Corinthians not to receive the grace of God in vain. This they might do by failing to accept and appropriate this grace, by refusing the gospel Paul proclaimed, or by not so living as to show that they had accepted the grace of God in Christ and were constrained by his love.

Paul enforces his appeal by a striking quotation from Isaiah (ch. 49:8). The prophet had spoken of a time when God would hear those who cried for help and would deliver those in need of salvation. Such a time had now come. This gospel dispensation, this era of grace, was the "accepted time"; it was "the day of salvation." The common interpretation, making "now" refer to the present moment, and declaring that decision must be immediate and that delay is dangerous, is not the exact meaning here. The message is rather that Paul and his readers are living in that blessed time which the prophet had foretold. Because God had provided salvation through his Son, because reconciliation had been accomplished, therefore the Corinthians should accept God's grace and take advantage of the full salvation which had been provided in Christ.

Of course the familiar application is allowable. Opportunities are not to be neglected. The part of the "day" granted to each individual is brief. Delay may be fatal. It may be true of anyone and at any time that the present day is the day, and the only "day of salvation."

Whatever his readers may do, however, Paul insists that his conduct is worthy of an ambassador of God. He is putting no stumbling block in the way of anyone. He is giving his readers no excuse for rejecting his message. He is giving no ground for ridiculing or criticizing his ministry. In everything he is approving himself, as all ministers should. The means of this approval are set forth in the verses which follow. In large measure they can serve as an ideal and give inspiration to all who are seeking to proclaim the gospel of grace.

To analyze and classify these twenty-eight phrases which characterize Paul's life as a minister may be difficult. However, the first ten set forth the endurance of physical suffering; the next eight, the manifestations of spiritual graces; the next three, Paul's conscious integrity amid conflicting criticisms; and the last seven, contrasted experiences which were reconciled in his ministry.

The first group of phrases begins with "patience," or steadfastness, or endurance; this is among the chief Christian virtues and describes one who has been tested, and who cannot be swerved from his course by any opposition or suffering. Nine particulars are then mentioned in which this "much patience," this great endurance, is shown.

Three forms of trouble which may be regarded as independent of human agency are mentioned: "afflictions," which might be avoided; "necessities," which are inevitable; "distresses," from which there is no escape.

Then follow three which are inflicted by men: "stripes"; "imprisonments"; "tumults," or the violence of mobs, as at Lystra and Thessalonica and Corinth itself.

The last three forms of suffering are such as Paul took upon himself in the fulfillment of his mission: "labors," which filled the day with weariness; "watchings," or vigils, which involved sleepless nights; and "fastings," which denote the hunger and thirst he endured in the accomplishment of his task. (Vs. 4-5.)

This list of sufferings prepares the way for the mention

of those virtues by which Paul proved himself to be a worthy ambassador of Christ. "Patience" was named, and then nine forms of trouble in which it was exercised. "Pureness," or the character of one who has a clean heart and clean hands, now heads a series of coordinate virtues: "knowledge" of divine things, or spiritual insight; "long-suffering," or forbearance which endures injuries and slights without resentment or anger; "kindness," the graciousness which puts others at ease and shrinks from giving pain; "the Holy Spirit," the source of all graces, or possibly "a spirit that is holy," as the mention of the divine Spirit would seem abrupt in this list of human virtues; "love unfeigned," unaffected, sincere; "the word of truth," or the proclamation of a pure gospel; and "the power of God," which was shown in all the results of Paul's missionary work. (Vs. 6-7.)

The next three clauses testify to the character of Paul's ministry in view of conflicting judgments of friends and foes. He was certain of his own integrity. Whether defending himself or rebuking others, he used only legitimate means and methods. Hence his conduct was approved "by the armor of righteousness on the right hand and on the left"; that is, by those weapons which righteousness supplied for the right hand or the left, offensive or defensive armor, as the sword for the right hand and the shield for the left.

This was true amid "glory and dishonor," whether he was receiving honor from his friends or ignominy from his foes; amid "evil report and good report," whether in his absence he was the object of calumny or of praise.

Paul ends the long list of phrases by a number of clauses in which he states in a series of striking contrasts the conditions of his ministry. The beauty and force of the passage lie in the fact that in each instance the opposites stated are both true, and both show him to be approved as a minister of God.

According to his enemies, and so, in the minds of many,

he and his associates were "deceivers," actual impostors, but they knew themselves to be "true."

In the judgment of contemptuous critics they were "unknown," obscure nonentities; yet by those capable of appreciating them they were "well known" and were given more and more recognition.

They were actually exposed to death; at any time their afflictions and sufferings might prove fatal. They are "dying," yet "behold" they "live," for Christ is ever giving them deliverance and new strength, and even when death actually comes it will issue for them in a life of endless glory.

They have been "chastened," but by the sufferings out of which God has brought blessing they have not been "killed." They were indeed "sorrowful," and overwhelmed with grief, yet "always rejoicing"; they were "poor" in material goods and as the world counted gains, "yet making many rich," with treasures of spiritual wealth.

They had "nothing," they had given even themselves to Christ; yet they were conscious of "possessing all things." Just because they belonged to Christ all things were theirs, and they held the whole world in their possession. (Vs. 8-10.)

By such credentials as these the apostle approved himself a minister of God; and in some measure every gospel messenger, and indeed every follower of Christ, should attest his sincerity and commend himself as an ambassador of the King.

E. THE APPEAL   Chs. 6:11 to 7:4

1. FOR SYMPATHY   Ch. 6:11-13

11 Our mouth is open unto you, O Corinthians, our heart is enlarged. 12 Ye are not straitened in us, but ye are straitened in your own affections. 13 Now for a recompense in like kind (I speak as unto my children), be ye also enlarged.

The success of a Christian minister depends upon his having the confidence and the love of his people. Such confidence Paul has been establishing in the opening chapters of this epistle. At least he has been giving his friends, who formed the majority of the Corinthian church, material to use in reply to the false teachers who had questioned his honesty. He has set forth his principles of action. This review of his ministry he closes with an appeal for sympathy and affection. He is not content with having his friends convinced of his sincerity; he wishes to be sure of their devotion and love.

This appeal for affection (ch. 6:11-13) is interrupted, however, by a warning to his readers to keep themselves separated from entangling alliances with idolaters (chs. 6:14 to 7:1), and the appeal is continued in the chapter which follows (ch. 7:2-4).

"Our mouth is open unto you, O Corinthians," writes the apostle. He has spoken with great frankness. He has revealed to them all the secret springs of his actions. Nothing has been kept back. He has laid bare before them all his motives and aims as a minister of Christ. Now he earnestly entreats them to show their sympathy and in return to treat him with a similar affectionate candor. "Our heart is enlarged." It has been expanded and stands wide open to receive them. If there exists any restraint or any lack of love, it is on their side, not on his. "Ye are not straitened in us, but . . . in your own affections." "Now for a recompense in like kind," to make a fair exchange and to give him what he has given (he is speaking to them as a loving father speaks to his children), they also should be "enlarged," and open their hearts in love to him.

Unrequited love is hard to bear. It had almost broken the apostle's heart to hear that the persons he had brought to Christ, for whom he had made every sacrifice, and whom he loved as his own spiritual children, had been led to doubt his sincerity and his integrity. Naturally, therefore, his careful explanation closes with this passionate appeal for affection.   (Vs. 11-13.)

2. FOR SEPARATION   Chs. 6:14 to 7:1

14 Be not unequally yoked with unbelievers: for what fellowship have righteousness and iniquity? or what communion hath light with darkness?   15 And what concord hath Christ with Belial? or what portion hath a believer with an unbeliever?   16 And what agreement hath a temple of God with idols? for we are a temple of the living God; even as God said, I will dwell in them, and walk in them; and I will be their God, and they shall be my people.   17 Wherefore
Come ye out from among them, and be ye separate, saith the Lord,
And touch no unclean thing;
And I will receive you,
18 And will be to you a Father,
And ye shall be to me sons and daughters,
saith the Lord Almighty.   1 Having therefore these promises, beloved, let us cleanse ourselves from all defilement of flesh and spirit, perfecting holiness in the fear of God.

Suddenly, however, he turns to solemn warning.   The frankness, the intimacy, the love which he requests for himself must not be shared with idolaters.   The followers of Christ must keep from all close alliances with those who have rejected Christ and allied themselves with an unbelieving world.

"Be not unequally yoked with unbelievers," writes the apostle.   He does not forbid all intercourse with them (see I Cor. 5:9-10; 7:12-13; 10:27), or those social and business contacts which may be necessary; but he warns against making such common cause with the pursuits and aims of unbelievers as might compromise Christian character and destroy the integrity and distinctness of Christian life.   His words are not to be applied only to marriages with unbelievers.   They should include all those intimacies which arise out of business relations, secret orders, social activities, friendships, and fellowships. Such intimacies, in themselves possibly innocent, may develop into unions which dwarf spiritual life, weaken loyalty to God, secularize the soul, and annul testimony to truth.

Paul enforces his warning by five argumentative questions, designed to show how unnatural, how incongruous, how unsafe such alliances should be considered.

The first four questions are united in pairs. The fifth, which mounts to the highest designation of Christian holiness, stands alone. The two moral and spiritual states are first contrasted: "What fellowship have righteousness and iniquity?" Coupled with this is the question contrasting the elements to which good and evil belong: "What communion hath light with darkness?"

Then the heads of the two opposing kingdoms are brought into contrast: "And what concord hath Christ with Belial?" The latter is supposed to be a designation of Satan. In the Old Testament the word is used to describe worthlessness, ruin, degenerate wickedness. Here it would mean that there can be no concord between divine purity and personified pollution.

The question which forms a couplet with this contrast marks the antithesis between the bonds uniting these supreme powers of good and evil with their subjects. These bonds are faith and unbelief. Thus Paul inquires, "What portion hath a believer with an unbeliever?"

The last question stands alone. It contrasts the forms of service to which these subjects were respectively devoted: "And what agreement hath a temple of God with idols?" The temple of God implies holiness. How can there be any assent between this sanctuary and the objects of idol worship, which are the very synonyms of impurity?

The apostle points to two great spheres of moral action, and he implies that there are only two. Every soul belongs to either the one or the other. He cannot belong to both. He has chosen the realm to which he will give allegiance. It is incongruous, it is inconsistent, it is fatal to follow any course of conduct which would attempt to unite the two.

Close fellowship with idolaters cannot but separate us from God.

"For we are a temple of the living God," writes the apostle. Not only is the heart of each believer such a sanctuary, but all believers together form such a temple, and they are encouraged to be true to God by the very promises of his divine indwelling.

Thus the apostle pleads with his readers to separate themselves from the idolatrous world in view of assurances made in the Old Testament: "I will dwell in them, and walk in them; and I will be their God, and they shall be my people."

This separation from the world was not to be physical and local and social, but moral and spiritual. These Corinthians were not to migrate to other cities, but to keep free from the intimacies and fellowships which might ally them with idolatry; and today Christians are to live in the world, while they are not of the world. They move among their fellowmen in close relationships, yet all the while they belong to another sphere of life. But this separation does not mean loneliness or loss. It results in a divine companionship which is more than compensation for all that the world offers. Such was the promise to God's people of old, and such is the assurance made to his servants today:

"Come ye out from among them, and be ye separate, saith the Lord,

And touch no unclean thing;

And I will receive you,

And will be to you a Father,

And ye shall be to me sons and daughters,
saith the Lord Almighty."

The soul of the Christian is ever being lurked back into the world, as Israel of old was ever turning to idolatry; but rest and satisfaction can be found only by turning again to God, for fellowship with whom the soul was created.

Paul closes his appeal with a precept which is both negative and positive: "Having therefore these promises, beloved, let us cleanse ourselves from all defilement of flesh and spirit, perfecting holiness in the fear of God." Negatively, the Christian is to put away not only every wrong action, but all thoughts and desires which may sully the whiteness of the soul. Then, positively, he must seek daily and continually for more perfect holiness; he must move toward the goal of absolute moral perfection, inspired by that "fear of God" which is born of a consciousness of his holy presence and of his unfailing love. (Chs. 6:14 to 7:1.)

3. For Affection   Ch. 7:2-4

2 Open your hearts to us: we wronged no man, we corrupted no man, we took advantage of no man. 3 I say it not to condemn you: for I have said before, that ye are in our hearts to die together and live together. 4 Great is my boldness of speech toward you, great is my glorying on your behalf: I am filled with comfort, I overflow with joy in all our affliction.

Suddenly Paul resumes his appeal for sympathy. He interrupted it by a solemn warning that intimacy and spiritual fellowship must be regarded as impossible between Christians and idolaters. However, between Christian friends affection is absolutely necessary if one is to be of real service to another. "Open your hearts to us," writes Paul; "make room for us in your affections. You have no reason to doubt or hesitate, we wronged no man, we corrupted no man, we took advantage of no man." He does not say this to condemn them, as though they had been the source of such accusations. Far from condemning them, he feels for them the deepest sympathy: "Ye are in our hearts to die together and live together." Neither death nor life can separate them from his love. In them he has the greatest confidence. In them he takes the greatest pride. Because of their friendship he is "filled with comfort," is made to "overflow with joy," in spite of all his affliction.

It is thus he prepares his readers for the resumption of the personal narrative concerning his meeting with Titus, which, as he now continues it, will explain the source and cause of this great joy.

F. THE ASSURANCE   Ch. 7:5-16

1. OF COMFORT   Ch. 7:5-12

5 For even when we were come into Macedonia our flesh had no relief, but we were *afflicted on every side; without* were *fightings, within* were *fears.   6 Nevertheless he that comforteth the lowly, even God, comforted us by the coming of Titus;   7 and not by his coming only, but also by the comfort wherewith he was comforted in you, while he told us your longing, your mourning, your zeal for me; so that I rejoiced yet more.   8 For though I made you sorry with my epistle, I do not regret it: though I did regret it (for I see that that epistle made you sorry, though but for a season),   9 I now rejoice, not that ye were made sorry, but that ye were made sorry unto repentance; for ye were made sorry after a godly sort, that ye might suffer loss by us in nothing.   10 For godly sorrow worketh repentance unto salvation,* a repentance *which bringeth no regret: but the sorrow of the world worketh death.   11 For behold, this selfsame thing, that ye were made sorry after a godly sort, what earnest care it wrought in you, yea what clearing of yourselves, yea what indignation, yea what fear, yea what longing, yea what zeal, yea what avenging!   In everything ye approved yourselves to be pure in the matter.   12 So although I wrote unto you, I wrote not for his cause that did the wrong, nor for his cause that suffered the wrong, but that your earnest care for us might be made manifest unto you in the sight of God.*

The account of Paul's experiences at Troas and in Macedonia was abruptly interrupted. (Ch. 2:12-13.) It is now as abruptly resumed. All that has intervened (chs. 2:14 to 7:4) may be regarded as a digression. In it Paul has set forth the nature and motives of his ministry. He now continues the narrative of what had befallen him in Macedonia, where he met Titus and received the favorable news from Corinth.

In spite of sudden transitions all these seven chapters of the epistle are bound together by a certain unity. The great theme is the sincerity of Paul. This had been denied by his enemies. Therefore, in writing to his friends in the church, the apostle sets forth his principles of action. He explains the delay in his approaching visit, and the change in his attitude toward an offending member. He records his deep anxiety for the state of the church, which was so great that, failing to meet Titus at Troas as he had expected, he hastened on to Macedonia. Here his anxiety was relieved by the favorable report from Titus. The remembrance of his joy leads him to speak of the triumphant character, and thus of other features, of his ministry. Even if this description is a digression, it is quite relevant. It shows the integrity of Paul's character and the sincerity of his motives. It closes with an appeal for sympathy and affection, and an expression of comfort and joy.

The personal narrative, which is resumed, explains the cause of this joy and the ground for the assurance of comfort (vs. 5-12), and of confidence (vs. 13-16), with which this section of the epistle ends.

" 'For even when we were come into Macedonia,' whither we had come when we had failed to meet Titus in Troas, 'our flesh had no relief.' " The word "flesh" is used here in its popular not in its technical sense, as the sphere not of sin but of suffering.

"We were afflicted on every side"; at every turn there was something to distress. "Without were fightings," wranglings, bitter conflicts for and against me; "within were fears," haunting anxiety as to how it all would end.

"Nevertheless he that comforteth the lowly," or rather, the dejected, the depressed, those that are cast down, "even God, comforted us by the coming of Titus." Not only did his fellowship with Titus cheer the apostle, but also the report of the comfort which the Corinthians had given to Titus, their desire to be reconciled with Paul, their sorrow for the trouble they had occasioned him, and their eagerness to support his cause. All this good news increased his joy.

He could hardly regret the pain which his former letter had occasioned the Corinthians. In fact he was very glad, not because they had suffered pain, but because their pain had resulted in repentance. For they had suffered "after a godly sort"; that is, as God would have men suffer, namely, so as to be led by suffering to a place of penitence. God had not caused the pain; it had been occasioned by the apostle's letter; but it was God's way and God's will that the suffering should issue in repentance, not that the apostle should work them any harm. "For godly sorrow worketh repentance unto salvation, a repentance which bringeth no regret: but the sorrow of the world worketh death." The former sorrow is that which feels pain because of the guilt of sin as an offense against God; the latter feels pain because of the consequences of sin. The contrast is between repentance and remorse, between the experiences of Peter and of Judas. The "sorrow of the world" is not sorrow for sin but chagrin at being found out and self-pity for the suffering which has been endured. Such worldly sorrow results only in "death," or moral ruin.

Paul points out the beneficial results of such "godly sorrow" in the case of the Corinthians. "For behold, . . . what earnest care it wrought in you," in contrast with former indifference; "what clearing of yourselves," by showing that the offender has not been shielded or his offense condoned; "what indignation," at the disgrace brought upon the church; "what fear" of consequences; "what longing" for the apostle's forgiveness and for his

return; "what zeal" to discipline the offender; "what avenging," what severity, in his punishment.   In every one of
these points the Corinthians had approved themselves,
and had shown that they were purged from all complicity
in the sin and no longer felt any guilty sympathy with the
offender.

Paul goes on to say that, as a matter of fact, his main
purpose in writing was not merely to secure the discipline
of the offender but to call forth an expression of the deep
concern, the "earnest care," which the Corinthians felt
for him. He wanted them to realize how much they really
cared for his sympathy, his goodwill, his love. It would be
difficult to imagine a more delicate way of expressing the
apostle's gratification at the obedience shown in response
to his severe and merited rebuke.   After all his anxiety
for them, he can assure his readers of the comfort which
now fills his heart.   (Vs. 5-12.)

2. OF CONFIDENCE   Ch. 7:13-16

13 Therefore we have been comforted: and in our com-
fort we joyed the more exceedingly for the joy of Titus,
because his spirit hath been refreshed by you all. 14 For
if in anything I have gloried to him on your behalf, I was
not put to shame; but as we spake all things to you in truth,
so our glorying also which I made before Titus was found
to be truth. 15 And his affection is more abundantly to-
ward you, while he remembereth the obedience of you all,
how with fear and trembling ye received him. 16 I rejoice
that in everything I am of good courage concerning you.

Last of all, Paul expresses his assurance of the mutual
confidence existing between himself and the members of
the Corinthian church.   He has been comforted by their
conduct and by the consciousness that his severe rebuke
had resulted only in the good he had intended. Yet over
and above his own comfort he was "the more exceedingly"
glad at the joy of Titus, whose spirit had been so refreshed

by their treatment of him.   Titus had accepted a delicate mission in going to Corinth.   Paul had tried to encourage him by praising the Corinthians and assuring him that in spite of their faults they were sound at heart.   He is now able to say that his praise of them was fully justified by their treatment of Titus.   He had not been "put to shame" by being shown to have made false statements in reference to them.   On the contrary, everything he had said to Titus of them had been "found to be truth," as was the case with all his statements.

As a result Titus shares with Paul a deeper affection than before his visit, as he recalls how the Corinthians obeyed the commands of the apostle and received his delegate "with fear and trembling."   Thus Paul can close with a joyful assurance that in every particular they sustained his confidence in them.   "I rejoice that in everything I am of good courage concerning you."

Thus, so far as possible, Paul's reconciliation with the Corinthians is complete.   The strong passion which has been moving through these opening chapters of the epistle subsides.   Paul's expression of confidence in his readers is like a calm after the storm, and it prepares the way for the following exhortation to them to show liberality to their fellow Christians in Judea.

II
THE COLLECTION FOR THE POOR CHRISTIANS AT JERUSALEM
Chs. 8; 9

A. THE EXAMPLE   Ch. 8:1-6

1 Moreover, brethren, we make known to you the grace of God which hath been given in the churches of Macedonia; 2 how that in much proof of affliction the abundance of their joy and their deep poverty abounded unto the riches of their liberality. 3 For according to their power, I bear witness, yea and beyond their power, they gave *of their own accord, 4 beseeching us with much entreaty in regard of this grace and the fellowship in the ministering to the saints: 5 and* this, *not as we had hoped, but first they gave their own selves to the Lord, and to us through the will of God. 6 Insomuch that we exhorted Titus, that as he had made a beginning before, so he would also complete in you this grace also.*

The eighth and ninth chapters of The Second Epistle of Paul to the Corinthians form the great classic passage on Christian beneficence. All the principles which should control Christian giving are here set forth. It is a complete summary of the motives and methods of church support and of church benevolences. If modern Christians were familiar with these principles and were guided by these instructions of the apostle, there never would be need of special appeals, and the treasuries of all boards and agencies of benevolence would overflow.

The occasion of these chapters was Paul's desire to

have the Christians in Corinth complete a collection for the relief of their fellow believers residing in Jerusalem. Just why there was such need for this Palestine relief fund is not stated. Possibly the Christians in Jerusalem were in financial straits because they practiced a community of goods. However, this experiment of Christian communism was not universal among them. It was purely voluntary. It obtained only for a time and was not observed by many of the wealthier members of the church.

More probably the poverty among the Christians in Jerusalem was due to the fact that the church in that city was composed largely of persons of small means, of tradesmen and artisans. Moreover, the Christians in that city were from the first subjected to persecution and to social ostracism which made it difficult for them to earn a livelihood.

Whatever the occasion of their poverty, it was obviously acute, and the rest of the Christian church felt sympathy for these fellow believers in Jerusalem who were suffering from this dire financial distress.

It was for the relief of these sufferers that Paul was concerned in making a collection. In this matter he had taken the keenest interest. There were a number of reasons why he was so eager for its success. First of all, the common grace of Christian charity would lead him to sympathize with persons in need. Then again, these particular persons were Jewish Christians, his kinsmen after the flesh, and his brethren in Christ. In the third place, it should be remembered that at the Council in Jerusalem, when it was agreed that Paul should be recognized as the apostle to the Gentiles, it had been specially stipulated that he should "remember the poor," by which was meant the "poor saints in Jerusalem." There was a fourth reason for his interest in this contribution: Such a gift from Gentile churches would prove, to any who were skeptical among the Jewish Christians, the reality and genuineness of the faith and the conversion of the Gentiles. Probably the supreme reason, however, was the desire of the apostle to establish the union of Jew and Gentile in the one body of Christ. Nothing would more clearly demonstrate such oneness of life than would this expression of sympathy and of love, given by converts from various nations to the members of the mother church in Jerusalem.

The motive for the treatment of this subject in these two chapters of this epistle was Paul's desire to have the Corinthian Christians complete their part of the collection before he reached the city. He was on his way and was passing southward through Macedonia when Titus met him with good news from Corinth. Among other important matters he learned that the members of the Corinthian church had begun to make their contribution at least a year earlier. Their interest had lapsed, or their minds had been diverted by the dissensions and difficulties in their church life. Therefore, as the apostle writes to prepare for his imminent coming, he devotes this second section of his letter to a presentation of the cause which is so dear to his heart. His approach to the subject is most courteous and happy. The previous portion of the epistle had closed with the statement of his joy and his confidence in his Corinthian friends. He begins this portion by telling them of the joy which has been occasioned by the generosity of the Macedonian Christians, among whom he is briefly sojourning, and by implying that as he has such confidence in the Corinthian Christians he can without fear broach the delicate subject of a church collection.

As a basis for the appeal which forms the substance of this section, he first describes the generosity of the Macedonian churches. "We make known to you," he writes, "the grace of God which hath been given in the churches of Macedonia." This grace, as he implies, has been and is still operating there. Its result is the production in the converts of an extraordinary degree of Christian generosity. As Paul states, "In much proof of affliction the abundance of their joy and their deep poverty abounded unto the riches of their liberality." By their "affliction" the apostle meant some particular persecution or distress which he was witnessing while among them. Its particular character is uncertain. Such sufferings were all too common among the Christians of the early church. In connection with this affliction the apostle mentions "the abundance of their joy." This is a striking combination of ideas, quite characteristic of the experiences in the early church. Suffering and joy were usually united. It is of peculiar interest to note that Paul was at this time in Macedonia, probably in Philippi. In this city he had sung his songs in the night, when he lay bleeding in the prison, and to these Macedonian believers he had written his great hymn of joy, namely, his Epistle to the Philippians. This he had penned while a prisoner in Rome.

In addition to their "affliction," Paul makes mention of "their deep poverty." This also was an experience with which the members of the early church were only too well acquainted. It is true, however, that Macedonia felt in a peculiar measure the oppression of Roman rule, and that as a colony it was continually complaining of its commercial difficulties and its financial straits. What Paul tells his Corinthian readers is that the test of affliction and the pitiful poverty issued in a rich stream of liberality. This last word originally meant simplicity or simple-mindedness. It seems to have meant that singleness of purpose which is directed toward the relief of others, with no selfish thought and no ulterior motive in mind; hence the word came to denote, as it does here, generosity or liberality. If "sincerity" is the word which embodies the message of the first seven chapters of this letter, liberality is the term which states the theme of the eighth and ninth chapters.

Paul declares of these Macedonian believers that "according to their power, . . . and beyond their power, they gave of their own accord." That is, their giving was not only in accordance with their means, but it went far beyond the limits of their slender resources, and, furthermore, it was purely voluntary and spontaneous; it was "of their own accord."

These Christians had shown their liberality still further in that, without waiting for any suggestion from the apostle, they had begged him as a special favor to allow them the privilege of having a part in the offering which was to be devoted to the relief of their fellow Christians in Jerusalem. He adds that they had increased his surprise by the spirit which they had shown. Not only had they given much more than he had expected, but they had given themselves to the Lord first of all, and then as servants to Paul, through whom their gifts were to be sent. It was this self-surrender which formed the chief feature of the grace which God had bestowed upon them. It was the most striking characteristic of their liberality.

The consequence of this self-dedication of the Macedonians to God and to his apostle was this very message which Paul was writing. He was sending it by the hand of Titus. He was commissioning this trusted friend to return at once to Corinth, and there to complete the task which he had begun on his recent visit. Or, as Paul expressed it in writing to these Corinthians, he had "exhorted Titus, that as he had made a beginning before, so he would also complete in you this grace also."

In reviewing this picture of the exemplary generosity of the Macedonian Christians, and in studying the instructions which follow, it should be noted that while Paul is referring to a church collection he never uses the word "money," but employs such felicitous phrases as a "grace," a service or "ministering," a communion in service or a "fellowship in ministering," a munificence or "bounty," a "blessing" (margin, ch. 9:5), a manifestation or "proof of love."

All these phrases are beautiful and full of meaning. Possibly the first is most significant of all. Liberality, according to the apostle, is a grace. Generosity is an endowment. It is a gift from God. It is a talent. By some it is possessed in a very striking degree, while others are almost as notable for their lack of this grace. However, like all talents, it may be cultivated. It is well for each believer to exercise this gift to the full extent of his ability, and it is sometimes stimulating for one to observe the liberality of others. Particularly does the example of persons who are in poverty, like these Macedonians, arouse others to generosity.

The Macedonians show some of the characteristics which, in greater or less degree, every Christian should manifest. In the face of every demand for relief, in answer to every appeal of suffering and want, there should be a response showing something of the joyousness, of the sacrifice, of the spontaneity, of the self-surrender, manifested by these largehearted members of the Macedonian church.

B. THE EXHORTATION   Ch. 8:7-15

7 But as ye abound in everything, in faith, and utterance, and knowledge, and in all earnestness, and in your love to us, see that ye abound in this grace also. 8 I speak not by way of commandment, but as proving through the earnestness of others the sincerity also of your love. 9 For ye know the grace of our Lord Jesus Christ, that, though he was rich, yet for your sakes he became poor, that ye through his poverty might become rich. 10 And herein I give my judgment: for this is expedient for you, who were the first to make a beginning a year ago, not only to do, but also to will. 11 But now complete the doing also; that as there was the readiness to will, so there may be the completion also out of your ability. 12 For if the readiness is there, it is acceptable according as a man hath, not according as he hath not. 13 For I say not this that others may be eased and ye distressed; 14 but by equality: your abundance being a supply at this present time for their want, that their abundance also may become a supply for your want; that there may be equality: 15 as it is written, He that gathered much had nothing over; and he that gathered little had no lack.

Having put the picture of the Macedonians before them, Paul now exhorts the Corinthians to manifest an equal generosity. His introduction is kindly and conciliatory. He compliments them on the rich supply of Christian graces which they have shown, and he intimates that it would be well if they abounded also in the grace of liberality. "But as ye abound in everything, in faith, and utterance, and knowledge, and in all earnestness, and in your love to us, see that ye abound in this grace also."

These graces which Paul mentions were all regarded as gifts of the Spirit. The very "faith" to which he refers was a special inducement. The "utterance" was the gift of teaching and of public testimony. The "knowledge" was that of divine things. "All earnestness" indicates zeal of every right kind. By "your love to us," Paul probably meant "the love which unites your hearts with ours."

All these gifts may be possessed by Christians who never manifest the grace of liberality. In the case of many, faith is strong, speech is fluent, knowledge is extensive, zeal is unquestioned, love for friends is fervent, but there appears to be no genius for generosity when collections are being taken for poor saints beyond the seas.

As giving is a grace, and would cease to be such if done under compulsion, Paul does not command the Corinthians. He does not dictate to them. He merely mentions the liberality of the Macedonians so that, by holding before the Corinthians this example, he may prove the genuineness of their Christian love.

The mention of love as a motive for their generosity leads Paul to dwell on the supreme example of love, one which was never absent from his mind. He speaks of "the grace of our Lord Jesus Christ." Here was love and self-sacrifice in its highest expression. Before he came into the world Christ possessed all the glory of heaven and all the majesty of the Godhead. For our sakes he surrendered all. He became man. He took upon himself "the form of a servant." This he did that through his voluntary poverty we might be blessed, not only with spiritual riches, but with all the fullness of his salvation. As Paul reminds the Corinthians, "Though he was rich, yet for your sakes he became poor, that ye through his poverty might become rich."

After the mention of such an example of Christian love, Paul might well have commanded the Corinthians to manifest Christian charity. He is careful, however, not to command. He merely expresses an opinion: "Herein I give my judgment." He declares that to give advice and not to command is the proper way of dealing with believers such as they. For they were not only the first persons to act in this matter of the collection, but the first to be willing to act, and this as far back as the previous year. He, therefore, advises them to carry out their plan so that their willingness to act may be equaled by their promptness in completing the collection, so far at least as their minds will allow. For generosity in giving is tested by willingness rather than by wealth. If one is eager to share, God measures his approval of the gift by the means one may possess, "for if the readiness is there, it is acceptable according as a man hath, not according as he hath not."

Paul closes these words of kindly advice by stating another law relative to Christian benevolence. Giving to the relief of fellow Christians is a matter of mutual consideration. The apostle states that he is not proposing this collection to relieve others at the risk of distress to his Corinthian friends. Burdens must be equalized. Their abundance may supply at the present time the want of the Judean Christians, but the time may come when the latter may have the privilege of relieving the necessities of the Christians in Corinth. The principle of equality should be maintained.

To illustrate this fact Paul quotes from the experience of the Children of Israel. When they gathered manna each morning on their wilderness journey, it is written, "He that gathered much had nothing over; and he that gathered little had no lack." In the case of Israel, it seems, this rule was carried out by some miraculous means, so that no one had more or less than he needed of the divine provision. In the case of Christians, the general principle will result, not in securing for each individual the exact amount of worldly goods which each other believer possesses, but in a situation where none will be in distress while others know the need and have the means to give relief. Such is the principle which Paul intimates the Corinthians may apply, as he reminds them again, not by way of command but of advice, of the distress which is to be met by this ministry to the members of the mother church in Jerusalem.

C. THE MESSENGERS   Chs. 8:16 to 9:5

16 But thanks be to God, who putteth the same earnest care for you into the heart of Titus. 17 For he accepted indeed our exhortation; but being himself very earnest, he went forth unto you of his own accord. 18 And we have sent together with him the brother whose praise in the gospel is spread *through all the churches; 19 and not only so, but who was also appointed by the churches to travel with us in* the matter of *this grace, which is ministered by us to the glory of the Lord, and* to show *our readiness: 20 avoiding this, that any man should blame us in* the matter of *this bounty which is ministered by us: 21 for we take thought for things honorable, not only in the sight of the Lord, but also in the sight of men. 22 And we have sent with them our brother, whom we have many times proved earnest in many things, but now much more earnest, by reason of the great confidence which* he hath *in you. 23 Whether* any inquire *about Titus,* he is *my partner and* my *fellow-worker to you-ward; or our brethren,* they are *the messengers of the churches,* they are *the glory of Christ. 24 Show ye therefore unto them in the face of the churches the proof of your love, and of our glorying on your behalf.*

1 For as touching the ministering to the saints, it is superfluous for me to write to you: 2 for I know your readi-

ness, of which I glory on your behalf to them of Macedonia, that Achaia hath been prepared for a year past; and your zeal hath stirred up very many of them. 3 But I have sent the brethren, that our glorying on your behalf may not be made void in this respect; that, even as I said, ye may be prepared: 4 lest by any means, if there come with me any of Macedonia and find you unprepared, we (that we say not, ye) should be put to shame in this confidence. 5 I thought it necessary therefore to entreat the brethren, that they would go before unto you, and make up beforehand your aforepromised bounty, that the same might be ready as a matter of bounty, and not of extortion.

Trust funds must be administered with scrupulous care. Particularly is this true when such funds represent gifts of the poor which have been sacrificed for the relief of those who are in even deeper distress. This care is to be exercised with a view not merely to efficiency but also to the preclusion of any possible suspicion of dishonesty or waste.

Thus Paul showed great wisdom in appointing a delegation of distinguished Christians to receive the offerings which were being made for the suffering saints in Jerusalem, and to convey these offerings to those upon whom they were to be bestowed.

After intimating to the Christians that it would be becoming in them to complete the collection they had begun, Paul cordially commends to them the commissioners who are to care for their gifts.

First among them he mentions Titus, the trusted friend, who had met him in Macedonia with the good news from Corinth. Paul thanks God for having put into the heart of Titus the same deep interest in the matter of this contribution which he himself feels. There is a delicate touch in the expression Paul uses as he refers to this contribution: "But thanks be to God, who putteth the same earnest care for you into the heart of Titus." The interest of Titus in the contribution is thus designated as "care"

for the Corinthians. They might think the concern of
Titus for the relief fund was zeal on behalf of the poor
saints in Jerusalem; it was really on behalf of the Corinthians. They would be the chief losers if they failed to
contribute generously to this fund.

Titus is said to have accepted gladly his new commission. Indeed, he had needed no request. He was so full
of enthusiasm for the cause that of his own unprompted
choice he was setting out to go to them.

As his colleague, Paul is sending with him "the brother
whose praise in the gospel is spread through all the
churches." Just who this fellow Christian was, it is futile
to conjecture. To the Corinthians he was well known,
for his devoted service to the Christian faith had won for
him the praise of all believers. Not only had he been
lauded by all the churches, but he had been chosen by
them to travel with Paul and to assist him in the matter
of the collection, so that Christ might be honored and
Paul's responsibility might be lightened.

This appointment had Paul's full consent, for he wished
to make sure that no one should have any ground for
criticizing or suspecting his conduct in connection with the
administration of this charity. Paul aimed at doing what
was absolutely honest, "not only in the sight of the Lord,
but also in the sight of men."

Unhappily it was necessary for Paul to take such pre-
cautions. Even his pure life and innocent purposes were
not free from suspicion and slander. His enemies were
contemptible enough to intimate that his interest in the
collection was not unselfish and that there was something
suspicious about his zeal for the gathering of such large
sums. Surely if Paul needed to be on his guard, much
more do those today who are concerned with the administration of funds for benevolent and missionary causes.
They should welcome the appointment of capable trea-
surers and auditors, and skilled accountants; thus they
protect their own reputations and also safeguard the en-

terprises against any rumors of inefficiency, dishonesty, or fraud.

The third deputy whom Paul was sending to be entrusted with the contributions of the Corinthians was a "brother" who had "many times proved earnest in many things, but now much more earnest, by reason of the great confidence" which he had in the Corinthians. The name of this Christian brother it is impossible to determine. Paul had tested his fidelity frequently and in many ways, and he now found him more zealous in Christian service than ever, eager to go upon this mission to Corinth because of the high regard for the Corinthian church which Paul had inspired.

These three delegates, accordingly, the Corinthians could receive without hesitation or question. If any inquiry should be made about Titus, they could commend him as Paul's intimate colleague and fellow laborer in all that concerned the welfare of the Corinthian church. As to the other commissioners, it could be stated that they were specially chosen delegates of the churches. That should be enough to guarantee their standing and ability. Paul adds, however, that these men are an honor to their Master. They are "the glory of Christ."

He urges the Corinthians to receive them and to respond to their appeals so cordially and generously that all the churches, which will soon know of their mission, will rejoice in the proof of the sincere love animating the Corinthian brotherhood, and will rejoice because of their liberality and their loyalty to Christ. (Vs. 16-24.)

Thus Paul has set forth one reason for commissioning the messengers to Corinth. It is the very reason for appointing modern church committees and boards and agencies, namely, to provide against all suspicion of dishonesty and of misuse in the administration of benevolent funds.

There is, however, another important purpose to be served, namely, the securing of efficiency. Individual enterprises and independent organizations are commonly less economical and the results of their activities are usually less permanent and satisfactory than in the case of agencies in which large groups of churches unite.

Paul might have gone alone to Corinth and might have secured funds to be administered according to his own discretion, but he knew that donors would be far more willing and generous when assured that their gifts were to be entrusted to a group of competent and accredited men.

He had another related reason for sending a commission. He knew the offerings would be thus more promptly secured, and he earnestly desired to have the collection entirely completed before his arrival, so that his own energies could be devoted to the spiritual instruction of the church. The collection was important, but the edification of believers was of still greater concern.

This should ever be borne in mind. Church benevolences are not to be neglected or evaded. A church that does not give does not live. Yet it is conceivable that a church may so absorb its time and energies in the collection of funds as to neglect the cultivation of its spiritual life. The two are inseparable, but the former should never be allowed to displace the latter.

In urging the Corinthians to complete their collection before his arrival, Paul appeals almost playfully to their pride. In this matter of "ministering to the saints" in Jerusalem, it is "superfluous" for him to write to such persons as themselves, for he well knows their eager interest. He has been boasting about them to the Macedonians, telling them that these Achaian Christians have been enthusiastic about the matter for more than a year. In fact the report of their zeal has aroused many of the Macedonians to give liberally to the cause. He is now sending Titus and his companions to prove that his praise was not an empty boast when he claimed for them such a readiness to give. He has been anxious to test and to justify this claim. For it would be a calamity if the Macedonians who might accompany him should find that the Corinthians were not ready to participate in this contribution. That would be decidedly embarrassing to him, and also to them in whom he had expressed such great confidence.

To avoid this possible discredit he has deemed it necessary to entreat these three brethren to go on in advance and to collect this promised bounty in good season. He wishes it to be a bounty, a real gift of love, and not something which may seem to have been extorted from them.

It would be well if the members of the modern church were so carefully instructed in the principles of stewardship and so intelligently interested in benevolent causes that no emotional appeals on special occasions would be necessary, but that the agents of missionary and other organizations would find them so ready to give that contributions would ever be in reality freewill offerings, gifts of love.

D. THE ENCOURAGEMENT   Ch. 9:6-15

6 But this I say, *He that soweth sparingly shall reap also sparingly; and he that soweth bountifully shall reap also bountifully.* 7 Let *each man* do *according as he hath purposed in his heart: not grudgingly, or of necessity: for God loveth a cheerful giver.* 8 *And God is able to make all grace abound unto you; that ye, having always all sufficiency in everything, may abound unto every good work:* 9 *as it is written,*

He hath scattered abroad, he hath given to the poor;
His righteousness abideth for ever.

10 *And he that supplieth seed to the sower and bread for food, shall supply and multiply your seed for sowing, and increase the fruits of your righteousness:* 11 *ye being enriched in everything unto all liberality, which worketh through us thanksgiving to God.* 12 *For the ministration of this service not only filleth up the measure of the wants of the saints, but aboundeth also through many thanksgiv-*

ings unto God;   13 seeing that through the proving of you
by this ministration they glorify God for the obedience of
your confession unto the gospel of Christ, and for the lib-
erality of your contribution unto them and unto all;   14
while they themselves also, with supplication on your be-
half, long after you by reason of the exceeding grace of God
in you.   15 Thanks be to God for his unspeakable gift.

Some have felt that in commending to the Corinthians
the commissioners who were to receive their contributions
Paul did not appeal to the highest motives. He induced
the Macedonians to contribute liberally by representing
the generosity of the Corinthians, and then he turned
about and urged the Corinthians to renew their generosity
by picturing to them the example of liberality shown by
the Macedonians. Further he urged the Corinthians to
contribute generously to the relief fund to save him from
embarrassment because he had boasted to others of their
liberality and did not wish to have his statements proved
to be untrue. However, under the conditions, the appeals
of the apostle were probably justifiable.

As Paul closes his message in relation to the collection
for the suffering Christians in Jerusalem, he presents motives which not only were pertinent to the Corinthians
but which are applicable to Christians in every age. First
of all, he encourages the Corinthians to be generous in
their gifts because of the enrichment certain to result in
their own lives. "But this I say, He that soweth sparingly
shall reap also sparingly; and he that soweth bountifully
shall reap also bountifully." This is a law of nature which
applies in every experience of life. One who scatters but
a little seed reaps but a small harvest, while generous sowing prepares for a harvest of abundant fruitage. Charity
is thus not a casting away, but a sowing. It is in the truest
sense an investment. It is certain to secure returns. Not
only does one who gives "lay up . . . treasures in
heaven," but he prepares to reap a harvest here on earth.

Of course charity cannot be commercial. It ceases to

be charity when exercised with a view to a reward. Nor yet can it be by compulsion. The charitable man must do "according as he hath purposed in his heart." His action must be in accordance with his own free will and desire; it must not be performed grudgingly, with sorrow and regret, "or of necessity," under the compulsion of circumstances, or the fear of criticism, or the custom of his society. "God loveth a cheerful giver." It is not the amount given which determines his approval, but the spirit of the one who gives; and one can safely trust in God.

It is usually in accordance with God's providential plan to increase the resources of the cheerful giver. "God is able to make all grace abound unto you; that ye, having always all sufficiency in everything, may abound unto every good work." He is able, and it is his wont, to grant to those who are liberal ample means, so that they may always have enough for any emergency of their own, and ample besides for the relief of others. This gracious provision is in accordance with the words of the psalmist:

"He hath scattered abroad, he hath given to the poor;
    His righteousness abideth for ever."

So it was the experience of the Old Testament believer to find that charity was a sowing which met the approval of God and the blessing of God, but which also resulted in a fruitage which would abide.

A similar experience may be expected by the follower of Christ. "He that supplieth seed to the sower and bread for food, shall supply and multiply your seed for sowing, and increase the fruits of your righteousness: ye being enriched in everything unto all liberality." This is a definite statement that those who give liberally may usually expect that their opportunities and their means for charity will be increased. They will be enriched on all occasions, so that they can be generous at all times. The rule is not without exceptions, but it is so general as to furnish encouragement in the exercise of this Christian grace of charity.

The cheerful giver is always spiritually enriched and usually is given increasing ability to exercise this grace.

Among the fruits of righteousness which result from liberal giving Paul mentions a second upon which he does not dwell. It is too obvious. The one who gives reaps a harvest in his own life, but his charity evidently bears fruit in the lives of those whom he relieves. Thus, in speaking of the contribution for the needy Christians in Jerusalem, Paul encourages generosity by stating that "the ministration of this service" would fill up "the measure of the wants of the saints." It does, indeed, aid one to be cheerful in giving when he pictures to himself the poverty and pain and anxiety which his gifts are certain to relieve.

The third result of charity which Paul mentions in order to encourage generosity on the part of the readers is the thanksgiving which their gifts will call forth. He indicates that a great chorus of praise would be evoked by their liberality. It would result in "many thanksgivings unto God."

This gratitude would be upon two grounds. First of all, the recipients would rejoice in such a manifestation of Christian sympathy. They would offer thanksgiving "for the liberality of your contribution unto them and unto all." The particular cause for their joy, however, would be the proof which this contribution from Gentile Christians would furnish of the reality and sincerity of their faith and their loyalty to their confession of the gospel of Christ.

This was a matter of deep concern to the apostle. This was, indeed, one of the main purposes in securing the contribution for the believers in Jerusalem. He wished the latter to be convinced of the genuineness of Gentile believers, and he wished both Jews and Gentiles to realize and to express their unity in Christ.

It is this last phase of the matter with which Paul closes his encouraging appeal. The Judean Christians would not only unite in thanking God for the love of their Gentile friends, but they would intercede for them at the throne of grace. They would unite in "supplication" on behalf of the Corinthian Christians, recognizing "the exceeding grace of God" manifested in them.

It is in view of this blessed result that Paul bursts forth in a closing doxology: "Thanks be to God for his unspeakable gift." There are many who feel that these words can only be interpreted as a direct reference to Christ, "the gift of God." It may be, however, that those are right who connect this phrase more directly with the thoughts which immediately precede. Paul has been so eager to have Jewish and Gentile believers put aside the enmities and prejudices which separated them that his heart overflows with gratitude as he pictures to himself the results in harmony and affection, in sympathy and love, which would issue from a gift of notable generosity offered by Gentile believers to their Jewish brethren in Christ. This would be a precious boon, the worth of which could not be expressed in words.

According to either interpretation the cause of thanksgiving to God would be the unutterable grace and goodness which he had manifested through his Son. Christ was the Gift of God's love. In him is found the true motive for all charity. He is the final Embodiment and Source of all grace, and for him thanks should be given to God, who is the Giver of every good and perfect gift.

PAUL'S DEFENSE OF HIS APOSTOLIC AUTHORITY

Chs. 10:1 to 13:10

A. THE DIVINE POWER   Ch. 10

1. ITS EXERCISE   Ch. 10:1-11

1 Now I Paul myself entreat you by the meekness and gentleness of Christ, I who in your presence am lowly among you, but being absent am of good courage toward you: 2 yea, I beseech you, that I may not when present show courage with the confidence wherewith I count to be bold against some, who count of us as if we walked according to the flesh. 3 For though we walk in the flesh, we do not war according to the flesh 4 (for the weapons of our warfare are not of the flesh, but mighty before God to the casting down of strongholds); 5 casting down imaginations, and every high thing that is exalted against the knowledge of God, and bringing every thought into captivity to the obedience of Christ; 6 and being in readiness to avenge all disobedience, when your obedience shall be made full. 7 Ye look at the things that are before your face. If any man trusteth in himself that he is Christ's, let him consider this again with himself, that, even as he is Christ's, so also are we. 8 For though I should glory somewhat abundantly concerning our authority (which the Lord gave for building you up, and not for casting you down), I shall not be put to shame: 9 that I may not seem as if I would terrify you by my letters. 10 For, His letters, they say, are weighty and strong; but his bodily presence is weak, and his speech of no account. 11 Let such a one reckon this, that, what we are in word by letters when we are absent, such are we *also in deed when we are present.*

The four closing chapters of Paul's second epistle to the Corinthians comprise a vindication of his authority as an apostle of Christ. These chapters differ so greatly in tone and spirit from the chapters which precede that they are supposed by many to form a separate epistle. It is concluded, indeed, that they constitute the severe letter of rebuke written before this second epistle and referred to in its opening section.

The contrast in tone, however, is sufficiently accounted for on the ground of the distinct purpose of this portion of the letter. In the earlier chapters Paul was addressing the great body of believers whom he regarded as his friends, and was endeavoring to remove from their minds certain suspicions which had been aroused as to his integrity and sincerity. In these closing chapters, without directly addressing them, he is rebuking bitter enemies who have cruelly assailed him and are endeavoring to undermine his influence and to corrupt his gospel. These enemies seem to have come from Jerusalem with letters, possibly spurious, from the mother church. They claimed to be true apostles and boasted some special relation to Christ. They seem to have belonged to that class known as Judaizers. They were attempting to combine the requirements of the Jewish law with the free grace of the gospel. Their motives were selfish and mercenary and their influence in the Corinthian church was becoming so great that Paul found it necessary to deliver this stern rebuke which has commonly been called his "great invective."

If the language is stern and passionate, Paul is not to be condemned as self-conscious and ill-tempered. He believes that the life of the Corinthian church is at stake. He speaks not with personal pique but as an apostle of Christ. He is not willing to allow the work of his Master to be destroyed by false teachers who have been attempting to corrupt the church.

It seems, also, that some Christians in Corinth had

fallen into grave moral faults.   Paul writes, in view of his
approaching visit, to rebuke the false leaders and to call
the offenders to repentance and reformation, so that on
his arrival he may be spared the painful necessity of exercising discipline.

The false teachers had accused Paul (*a*) of cowardly
weakness and lack of effectiveness, (*b*) of not possessing
a full knowledge of Christ and so of the true gospel, (*c*) of
accepting no salary because conscious that he was an
impostor.

The main portion of his defense, therefore, answers
these charges in order.

a. He claims divine power, which he will exercise if
necessary, and which is to be measured not by empty
boasts but by actual achievement.   (Ch. 10.)

b. He defends the pure gospel which he is proclaiming.   (Ch. 11:1-6.)

c. He gives his reason for refusing any remuneration
for his missionary labors.   (Ch. 11:7-15.)   He next states
the grounds on which he might boast and by which his
apostolic authority is vindicated.   (Chs. 11:16 to 12:10.)
Then, after expressions of personal love, he ends his defense by warning both the guilty members of the church
and the false teachers.   (Chs. 12:11 to 13:10.)

He begins with a personal and tender appeal, "Now I
Paul myself entreat you by the meekness and gentleness
of Christ."   These words are in striking contrast to the
severe and even bitter rebukes by which his defense is
characterized; but it must be noted that, however passionately he may attack his opponents, he never loses his self-
control, his sanity, or his consciousness that he is a servant of Jesus Christ.   Thus here he first of all calls to
mind the meekness and forgiving love of his Master.   He
intimates that these should be imitated by all who pro-
fess to be Christ's servants, and that they form his own
rule of action.

There is a special reason for thus directing attention to

himself and naming these virtues. He is beginning a defense which is intensely personal in answer to an attack
upon him due to a misinterpretation of the meekness and
gentleness which he showed when on a previous visit to
Corinth. His critics had declared that when he was present his conduct was cowardly and contemptible, but that
when he had left them he could write back letters which
were bold and fearless. It is the cruel sneer of his enemies which he quotes: "I who in your presence am lowly
among you, but being absent am of good courage toward
you." This unkind charge was probably supported by
the fact that he had shown himself to be mild and patient
when with them, but subsequently had written the brief,
severe letter. His conduct had been basely misconstrued
as weakness and cowardice, due to a conscious lack of
power and of divine authority. (V. 1.)

He now insists that he does possess an authority and a
power which he will exercise if necessary, but he entreats
them to spare him this sad necessity. "I beseech you,
that I may not when present show courage with the confidence wherewith I count to be bold against some, who
count of us as if we walked according to the flesh." There
are those then against whom he expects to proceed with
severity, but he hopes that the Corinthian Christians will
not be among that number. It is only against the false
teachers that he is planning to act with a "courage" and
"confidence" which will be shown in the severity of his
discipline.

These enemies have accused him of being one who
"walked according to the flesh." He retorts, "Though we
walk in the flesh, we do not war according to the flesh."
Here he is playing upon the word "flesh" and intimating
its contrary uses. He admits that he is conscious of human weakness and limitations, but he has not been guided
by human motives of cowardice and fear, "for," he says,
"though we walk in the flesh, we do not war according to
the flesh." (V. 3.)

The weapons by which he is waging his spiritual warfare are not worldly and carnal. They are not those of feeble human nature, but the mighty weapons which God has supplied for overthrowing the strongholds which defy his gospel. It is with such divine power that Paul is succeeding in "casting down imaginations, and every high thing that is exalted against the knowledge of God." The systems of human speculation, like the proud philosophies of Greece, since they are opposed to the truth which God has revealed, cannot stand before the power which has been committed to the apostle. It is able to make captive every rebellious thought and to bring it into submission and obedience to Christ. (Vs. 4-5.)

Whatever disobedience might exist in the Corinthian church, Paul was quite ready to show his power, to rebuke and to overcome it. But he wished to delay until the members of the church had fully established their willingness to obey him and then he would proceed against the false teachers, who were really those to be punished for their obstinacy and their rebellion against the authority of the apostle. (V. 6.)

He warns the Corinthians against being misled by appearances and by superficial judgments: "Ye look at the things that are before your face." They should look deeper. They should not be so easily misled by the foolish boasts of the false teachers. The latter claimed an exceptional and intimate relationship to Christ, and pretended to be his special messengers. It would be well for the Corinthians to consider such claims a little more carefully. They would then conclude that these teachers were arrogating to themselves nothing which Paul did not actually possess. "If any man trusteth in himself that he is Christ's, let him consider this again with himself, that, even as he is Christ's, so also are we." (V. 7.)

If Paul, indeed, should glory in his peculiar relation to the Master and in the authority and power which Christ had entrusted to him alone, it would be no idle boast; he would "not be put to shame" as an impostor when he reached Corinth. This authority and power had been entrusted to him for the edification of the Corinthian church, not for its destruction. The Lord had given these gifts "for building you up, and not for casting you down" (v. 8).

Unless absolutely necessary this authority will not be exercised in the way of punishment and discipline. More than this Paul will not say, lest he may seem to be attempting to overawe the Corinthians with written threats or to "terrify" them by his "letters." The contemptuous sneers of his enemies have been reported to him: "His letters, they say, are weighty and strong; but his bodily presence is weak, and his speech of no account." (V. 10.)

To this sneer Paul makes reply that anyone who talks in this way may rest assured that when Paul arrives he will express himself quite as forcibly by action as he does by letter when absent, "Let such a one reckon this, that, what we are in word by letters when we are absent, such are we also in deed when we are present." (V. 11.)

As to Paul's personal appearance much has been conjectured and is being popularly reported for which there is no basis in fact. He is described as an ugly little Jew, bald, squat of stature, bandy-legged, with bowed shoulders. Not only is he pictured as grotesque in appearance, but he is made contemptible as the alleged victim of humiliating infirmities, such as ophthalmia and epilepsy.

That he did suffer from some extreme physical affliction he is about to affirm. (Ch. 12:7-10.) That this "thorn in the flesh" was epilepsy, or that the personal appearance of the apostle was displeasing, it is as cruel as it is unnecessary to conjecture. The present passage contains no reflection upon his appearance. The sneer that "his bodily presence" was "weak, and his speech of no account" was not directed against any physical defects. It was intended to contrast his character and conduct when present in Corinth with the boldness and severity of his

letters written from a distance.   There may be a reference to the gentleness and forbearance shown on his last
visit, qualities which were mistaken for weakness and
cowardice, which as such were in striking contrast to the
brief, severe letter which had resulted in the repentance
and contrition of the church.   "This man," so said his
enemies, "is bold and firm enough when he writes, but
when he arrives he is timid in action and his speech is
beneath contempt."

It must be remembered that this was a false charge
which Paul resented.   He replies that when he returns, his
bodily presence and his speech will be just as full of energy and courage as are his letters.   Now if one were to
argue from this passage as to the personal appearance of
the apostle, the only possible conclusion would be that his
physical appearance was impressive, if not imposing, for
it was of the same character as his letters.

All this, however, is somewhat aside from the message
of the paragraph.   It contains on the part of the apostle
a claim to divine power.   This power was such that,
whatever the human instrument, it was sufficient to over-
throw all the strongholds of intellectual and spiritual pride
which stood opposed to the gospel and able to bring
"every thought into captivity to the obedience of Christ."
We are not to suppose that such power rested on Paul
alone.   A like power is ever granted in some measure to
all who seek to proclaim the gospel with like devotion to
their Lord.

2. ITS MEASURE   Ch. 10:12-18

*12 For we are not bold to number or compare ourselves
with certain of them that commend themselves: but they
themselves, measuring themselves by themselves, and comparing themselves with themselves, are without understanding.   13 But we will not glory beyond* our *measure, but
according to the measure of the province which God appor-*

tioned to us as a measure, to reach even unto you. 14 For we stretch not ourselves overmuch, as though we reached not unto you: for we came even as far as unto you in the gospel of Christ: 15 not glorying beyond our measure, that is, in other men's labors; but having hope that, as your faith groweth, we shall be magnified in you according to our province unto further abundance, 16 so as to preach the gospel even unto the parts beyond you, and not to glory in another's province in regard of things ready to our hand. 17 But he that glorieth, let him glory in the Lord. 18 For not he that commendeth himself is approved, but whom the Lord commendeth.

The meaning of this passage is somewhat concealed by its irony and sarcasm. Paul has been insisting that the charge of weakness and cowardice brought against him by his enemies is false. He here confesses that there is one form of courage he lacks. He does not dare to do as some people whom he knows. He has not the courage to boast a power he does not possess, or to claim a relation to Christ he has never known. He admits that he does not have the bravery to even put himself in their number, much less to compare himself with certain persons who are great only in their own admiration, and are distinguished for their commendation of themselves. These enemies of the apostle form a mutual admiration society. Their own achievements constitute their standard of excellence, and they congratulate themselves and one another on attaining this standard: "They themselves, measuring themselves by themselves, and comparing themselves with themselves, are without understanding." Such mutual admiration societies are popular down to the present day. They may be found even in religious circles. This attitude of mind, however, according to the apostle, does not indicate a very high order of intelligence. Such men are "without understanding." (V. 12.)

It would be a sign of much more sagacity if such self-satisfied admirers of their own achievements would compare themselves with others whose work is of some real significance.

The attainments of Paul's enemies had consisted merely in their intrusion into the field of his labors, and they were priding themselves only on the ground that they had stolen some of his converts. They would feel less like boasting if they compared their accomplishments with those of Paul, who had founded the church in Corinth.

For his own part, Paul will make no boast which goes beyond the limits of his actual work. He will confine himself to the limits of the province which God marked out for him, a province which includes Corinth and his converts in that city. (V. 13.)

He is not straining to exceed the limits of his province, as he would be doing if he had received no divine commission to come to Corinth. He was in the appointed sphere of his apostolic labors when he pressed on even to that city and was the first to proclaim there the gospel of Christ. (V. 14.)

Therefore, Paul's glorying in the work he had achieved did not go beyond legitimate bounds. Unlike the false teachers who were rejoicing in their attempts to corrupt the church he had established, he was not setting up claims to a work which other men had done. He was gratified in the results of his own efforts in Corinth. In fact he was hoping that, as the Christian devotion of his converts there increased, he might be able to expand the sphere of his apostolic labors, and aided by their support might be able to preach the gospel even in the unevangelized regions beyond Corinth. He did not wish to claim credit, as some people were doing, for work already accomplished within the field of service divinely appointed to another workman. (Vs. 15-16.)

However, in any case, Paul would take no credit to himself. He insisted that for a servant of Christ there can be only one ground of gratification, only one rule for the assertion of claims. It is not proud self-praise, but glorying in the grace of God by which all success is achieved. As the prophet has said, "But he that glorieth, let him glory in the Lord" (cf. Jer. 9:24). For he who, instead of giving all glory to God, commends himself, is not the man who is really approved, but he whom the Lord commends. (Vs. 17-18.)

Paul intimates that he is himself one who is glorying in the Lord. He is not praising himself. His power for service which his enemies are denying is a divine trust. The Lord has shown his approval of Paul, not of the false teachers, by the work he has accomplished through Paul in the church at Corinth.

B. THE GODLY JEALOUSY   Ch. 11:1-15

1. OF FALSE TEACHING   Ch. 11:1-6

1 Would that ye could bear with me in a little foolishness: but indeed ye do bear with me. 2 For I am jealous over you with a godly jealousy: for I espoused you to one husband, that I might present you as a pure virgin to Christ. 3 But I fear, lest by any means, as the serpent beguiled Eve in his craftiness, your minds should be corrupted from the simplicity and the purity that is toward Christ. 4 For if he that cometh preacheth another Jesus, whom we did not preach, or if ye receive a different spirit, which ye did not receive, or a different gospel, which ye did not accept, ye do well to bear with him. *5 For I reckon that I am not a whit behind the very chiefest apostles. 6 But though I be rude in speech, yet am I not in knowledge; nay, in every way have we made* this *manifest unto you in all things.*

No faithful worker can endure keener pain than that caused by seeing the fruit of his labors destroyed. This is particularly true when one is working with souls. Nothing can be more distressing than to learn that affection is being alienated, faith undermined, and beliefs corrupted.

It is, therefore, not difficult to understand the distress

felt by Paul when he saw the havoc which was being
wrought among the Corinthian believers by the false
teachers from Jerusalem.   In order to show the absurdity
of their claims, he has already referred to the success of
his own apostolic service, of which the Corinthian church
is a demonstration and a proof, and, further, a sign of
divine approval.   This claim on his part may sound like
boasting, but he knows no other way of meeting the self-
glorification of the false apostles who had so imposed on
the minds of the Corinthians.   He sees the necessity of
adopting their tactics.   He admits that it is a form of folly,
but he shows the reason for his action.   He apologizes to
his readers for a course which seems absurd, but he insists
that he adopts it because of his love for them.   "I hope
that you can endure a little foolish boasting on my part,"
he is saying.   "It is foolish to boast; but you stand a good
deal of it from certain other people, and I am sure that
you are forgiving me.   My reason for such folly is this:
I am jealous over you with a godly jealousy."   The boasting of the false teachers has beguiled his converts and
Paul must now imitate the folly to avert a disaster.   His
boasting, therefore, is not selfish.   It springs from his
jealous affection, from a love tormented by fear.   He is
not fearing, however, for his own reputation or personal
prestige.   God has put this jealousy in his heart.   It is
the work which God had done in the Corinthians that is
in danger of being destroyed, and his inheritance in them
which is in danger of being lost.   Paul had been acting as
a messenger of God.   His aim has been to secure for
Christ a church absolutely loyal to him: "I espoused you
to one husband, that I might present you as a pure virgin
to Christ."

It must be noted that Paul is referring here to the col-
lective church.   To speak of a single soul as a bride of
Christ introduces conceptions which are unscriptural and
misleading.   In bringing believers to submit to Christ as
Lord and Master, Paul had betrothed the church to Christ,

figuratively speaking, hoping that this church would prove to be faithful as a true bride to her one husband.

He is, however, tormented by fear. He is afraid that these false and pretentious teachers may lead the Corinthians away from their single-minded faithfulness to Christ, "as the serpent beguiled Eve in his craftiness." Nor are his fears groundless. It is exactly the purpose of these enemies that their "minds should be corrupted from the simplicity and the purity that is toward Christ." Of these deceivers the Corinthian Christians had been exceedingly tolerant. Some had come preaching "another Jesus," whom Paul did not preach, one who was not the Christ, the divine Son of God; and "a different spirit," which they had not received, not a spirit of freedom and of joy, but a spirit of bondage and of fear; also a "different gospel" from that which they had accepted, a system of ceremonies and works of supposed merit, not a message of free grace and redeeming love.

When such a preacher appeared, the Corinthians bore with him quite beautifully. The clause "Ye do well to bear with him" is intensely sarcastic. Paul's meaning seems to be this: "When such a teacher comes, your toleration of his vagaries is quite lovely"; and Paul implies the question, "Do you not think that you might show a little toleration to one like me, who has proved to you that he is a true apostle of Christ?" He adds, "For I reckon that I am not a whit behind the very chiefest apostles." By the latter he may refer to Peter and John or others of the Twelve. Much more probably his words are an ironical reference to the pretentious teachers who had imposed themselves on the Corinthian church, and the phrase may be translated, "I am not a whit behind these preeminent apostles," or "these precious apostles of yours."

He admits that in one particular he may be inferior to these teachers. He may be less eloquent than they; he may be untrained in oratory; he may not have their tricks of beguiling and falsifying speech. However, in his knowledge of divine things and of the essential truths of the gospel he is not lacking.   Of this he has given ample proof to the Corinthians in all his work among them.

Nothing can be more pitiful than to see men being turned away from the teachings of Paul.   Those who are being so misled are surely being taught another Jesus, another spirit, another gospel.   After all, it is the Christ whom Paul preached who is the Christ of God.

2. OF FEIGNED GENEROSITY   Ch. 11:7-15

7 Or did I commit a sin in abasing myself that ye might be exalted, because I preached to you the gospel of God for nought?   8 I robbed other churches, taking wages of them that I might minister unto you;   9 and when I was present with you and was in want, I was not a burden on any man; for the brethren, when they came from Macedonia, supplied the measure of my want; and in everything I kept myself from being burdensome unto you, and so will I keep myself.   10 As the truth of Christ is in me, no man shall stop me of this glorying in the regions of Achaia.   11 Wherefore? because I love you not?   God knoweth.   12 But what I do, that I will do, that I may cut off occasion from them that desire an occasion; that wherein they glory, they may be found even as we.   13 For such men are false apostles, deceitful workers, fashioning themselves into apostles of Christ.   14 And no marvel; for even Satan fashioneth himself into an angel of light.   15 It is no great thing therefore if his ministers also fashion themselves as ministers of righteousness; whose end shall be according to their works.

It is easy to misjudge others and to impute to them unworthy motives.   This is particularly true of men in public life.   Their actions are matters of common knowledge.   Their real motives are known to themselves alone.

In the case of Paul, nothing could be more contemptible and insincere than the charge brought against him by his enemies.   He had declined to accept any financial support from the Corinthians lest he might be suspected of mercenary motives.   The false teachers learned of his gen-

erosity and insisted that he received no remuneration because he knew that he was not a true apostle.

Paul has just declared in the preceding paragraph that
he is at least an equal of these false teachers whose pretentious claims have so impressed the Corinthian church.
He now refers to the slander these men have originated.
It may be that the Corinthians believe that Paul has for-
feited his claim to be an apostle by renouncing his right
to their support as he preached the gospel to them.   He
has always claimed this right.   In a previous epistle he had
maintained and defended it.   (I Cor. 9:14.)   Has he now
done wrong in resigning it?   Will the Corinthians allow
his enemies to lay hold of his self-denial as a weapon with
which to defeat him and to destroy his influence?   "Did
I commit a sin in abasing myself that ye might be exalted?"   Was it wrong for him to stoop to manual labor
in earning bread when he did so to raise his converts from
the degradation of idolatry?   He had made this sacrifice
in bringing them the priceless treasure of the gospel.

As a matter of fact, he has accepted support from other
churches in order to preach gratuitously to the Corinthians.   That was almost like robbery, yet he did so out
of consideration for them.   When at times his funds were
exhausted while at Corinth, when even by plying his trade
as a tentmaker he could not supply his needs, he refrained
from putting pressure on any Corinthian to aid in his support.   In one instance the Christian brethren who arrived
from Macedonia supplied his necessities by the gifts they
brought.   Under no conditions did he allow himself to
become burdensome to the church at Corinth and he was
resolved to continue the practice.   He vows by the very
truth of Christ which he proclaims that he will allow no
one in the regions of Achaia to deprive him of the glory
of preaching the gospel without compensation.

Do they wish to know his motive?   Is it lack of love for
the Corinthians?   Does he hesitate to put himself under
obligation to them as though he did not trust and respect

them? God knows this is not true. While at first it seemed wise to avoid arousing their suspicion of mercenary motives, yet now his purpose is different. He has in mind not the Corinthian church but the false teachers who are slandering him and misleading it. He wishes to cut the ground from under the men who desire a pretext for claiming that they work under the same conditions as he, both they and he receiving support from the church.

This gratuitous preaching is for him a real reason for glorying. He will not give it up, for by so doing he would afford an opportunity to his enemies for claiming to be as unselfish as he. His unselfishness is real; theirs is a deception and a mere pretense. He is unwilling to give them any opening. For they are sham apostles, their whole work is a fraud, while they put on an appearance of being "apostles of Christ." No wonder, for Satan himself, their real master, puts on, in his temptations of men, the guise of "an angel of light." It is not strange, therefore, that these his servants should pose as teachers of truth and ministers of righteousness. Such pretense will not avail. Their doom will be in accordance with their deeds.

Paul's severity is fully justified. Nothing is more diabolical than to ascribe evil motives to good actions. It was satanic to insinuate that Paul's self-sacrifice as an apostle was due to his consciousness of being an impostor. Men of evil minds are ever ready to misinterpret virtue as vice, while in their own lives they conceal vice under a mask of assumed virtue. Satan, the great accuser, still fashions himself into "an angel of light."

C. THE ENFORCED BOASTING
Chs. 11:16 to 12:10

1. THE NECESSITY   Ch. 11:16-21

16 I say again, Let no man think me foolish; but if ye do, yet as foolish receive me, that I also may glory a little. 17 That which I speak, I speak not after the Lord, but as in foolishness, in this confidence of glorying. 18 Seeing that many glory after the flesh, I will glory also. 19 For ye bear with the foolish gladly, being wise yourselves. 20 For ye bear with a man, if he bringeth you into bondage, if he devoureth you, if he taketh you captive, if he exalteth himself, if he smiteth you on the face. 21 I speak by way of disparagement, as though we had been weak. Yet whereinsoever any is bold (I speak in foolishness), I am bold also.

Is it ever right to boast? Not if by boasting is meant a proud rehearsal of personal possessions or attainments, made with a selfish view to securing popularity and praise. Sometimes, however, one may be impelled to recite his sufferings and sorrows and peculiar privileges, and to magnify the mercy and grace of God shown toward him, that the claims of enemies may be silenced and that the name of Christ may be glorified.

Paul found himself compelled to boast. His enemies forced him to adopt a weapon which was quite in accord with their character but most uncongenial to the apostle. By their proud pretensions they had captivated many in the Corinthian church. He felt that there was no way of rescuing his converts from their peril except to show himself as a divinely appointed apostle, superior to these vain pretenders. He has already shown that they have intruded into his sphere of activity by coming to Corinth, and that as the founder of the church he is worthy of more honor than those who seem intent upon corrupting the converts whom he has brought to Christ. He has further proved his surpassing generosity in declining the financial support which his rivals were sternly demanding. He is about to show that his labors and sufferings as an apostle have been far greater than theirs and that he has been granted revelations and spiritual experiences which no other man had ever known.

He first pauses, however, to vindicate or to excuse himself for the unusual course he is adopting. He is, indeed, compelled to boast, but it is to be under definitely understood conditions. It is to be the action of one who well knows that in itself boasting is mere folly, and that when adopted by him it must be regarded by his readers as something to be merely tolerated and not followed by them as an example. It is a method of defense to which he has been forced. It is not in accord with the example or the spirit of Christ. It is a boasting of infirmities and a glorifying of the grace of God.

Nevertheless, these admissions and explanations on the part of the apostle should not lead to the conclusion that he here takes a false step or that he is acting contrary either to his judgment or to his conscience. Here in fact is a master stroke of genius. By it Paul demonstrates the inanity of the pretensions made by the false teachers. He reveals facts in reference to his own life which his readers seem to have forgotten, and which the Christian world would otherwise never have known. Best of all, he attributes all to the power of Christ and shows how his grace can triumph over all weakness and be glorified even in extreme distress.

He begins this explanation of his course by again declaring that considered in itself boasting is folly: "I say again, let no one think me a fool for uttering what does sound so much like folly. But if you do regard me as such, yet bear with me that I, too, like my enemies, may boast a little. This method of speaking does not follow the example of Christ. He never boasted. Nor, unless demanded by necessity, would this be in accord with his spirit. But there is no other way open before me. In my 'confidence of glorying' I am merely answering fools according to their folly. Since your false teachers, from a selfish, worldly point of view, are urging upon you their claims, I am not at liberty to be wholly silent concerning my own. You Corinthians are so very wise yourselves that you can afford to bear with fools and you do so gladly. In your sublime tolerance, you are capable of bearing with any of these impostors, no matter what he does; whether he makes slaves of you, lives at your expense, entraps you, gives himself airs, strikes you in the face. If such conduct is a fair measure of strength, I admit with shame that I am too weak, just as my enemies say, to act in this way. Yet wherever real courage is in question (I resume my foolish boasting), I, too, have courage, and can match anyone in his claims."

To condemn Paul for his enforced boasting is as unnecessary as it is popular. However, it is certainly unwise for any Christian to attempt to follow his example, at least unless he is certain that his own labors and sufferings and revelations have been as great as those of the apostle and that his circumstances fully justify an endeavor to follow in Paul's unwonted course.

2. The Grounds   Chs. 11:22 to 12:10

22 Are they Hebrews? so am I. Are they Israelites? so am I. Are they the seed of Abraham? so am I. 23 Are they ministers of Christ? (I speak as one beside himself) I more; in labors more abundantly, in prisons more abundantly, in stripes above measure, in deaths oft. 24 Of the Jews five times received I forty stripes save one. 25 Thrice was I beaten with rods, once was I stoned, thrice I suffered shipwreck, a night and a day have I been in the deep; 26 in journeyings often, in perils of rivers, in perils of robbers, in perils from my countrymen, in perils from the Gentiles, in perils in the city, in perils in the wilderness, in perils in the sea, in perils among false brethren; 27 in labor and travail, in watchings often, in hunger and thirst, in fastings often, in cold and nakedness. 28 Besides those things that are without, there is that which presseth upon me daily, anxiety for all the churches. 29 Who is weak, and I am not weak? who is caused to stumble, and I burn not? 30 If I must needs glory, I will glory of the things that concern my weakness. 31 The God and Father of the Lord Jesus, he who is blessed for evermore knoweth that I lie not. 32 In Damascus the governor under Aretas the

*king guarded the city of the Damascenes in order to take
me: 33 and through a window was I let down in a basket
by the wall, and escaped his hands.*

*1 I must needs glory, though it is not expedient; but I
will come to visions and revelations of the Lord. 2 I know
a man in Christ, fourteen years ago (whether in the body,
I know not; or whether out of the body, I know not; God
knoweth), such a one caught up even to the third heaven.
3 And I know such a man (whether in the body, or apart
from the body, I know not; God knoweth), 4 how that he
was caught up into Paradise, and heard unspeakable words,
which it is not lawful for a man to utter. 5 On behalf of
such a one will I glory: but on mine own behalf I will not
glory, save in* my *weaknesses. 6 For if I should desire to
glory, I shall not be foolish; for I shall speak the truth: but
I forbear, lest any man should account of me above that
which he seeth me* to be, *or heareth from me. 7 And by
reason of the exceeding greatness of the revelations, that I
should not be exalted overmuch, there was given to me a
thorn in the flesh, a messenger of Satan to buffet me, that
I should not be exalted overmuch. 8 Concerning this
thing I besought the Lord thrice, that it might depart from
me. 9 And he hath said unto me, My grace is sufficient
for thee: for* my *power is made perfect in weakness. Most
gladly therefore will I rather glory in my weaknesses, that
the power of Christ may rest upon me. 10 Wherefore I
take pleasure in weaknesses, in injuries, in necessities, in
persecutions, in distresses, for Christ's sake: for when I
am weak, then am I strong.*

Paul is compelled to boast. In order to shame and
silence his enemies who deny his apostolic authority and
are endangering the life of the church, he feels it necessary
to give a recital of the labors and sufferings and spiritual
privileges by which his apostleship has been attested.

The passage forms a summary of Paul's career as an
apostle. As a sketch of his life written by himself, the
New Testament contains nothing to compare with it in
fullness and interest. It reveals what a small fragment
of his experiences are recorded by Luke in The Acts.

Luke was not writing a biography of Paul, but a history
of the founding of the Christian church. The Bible contains no life of the great apostle; those writers who, by
piecing together the historical fragments, have attempted
to produce such a life find more material in these few
verses than in the compass of any passage of equal length.
The story is here told with tantalizing brevity, and no one
can read the verses without a real longing for an enlarged
picture of the experiences here faintly sketched.

Paul begins with a reference to his descent. His enemies seem to boast of their relation as Jews to the mother
church in Jerusalem. In this regard they have no advantage over the apostle: "Are they Hebrews? so am I.
Are they Israelites? so am I. Are they the seed of Abraham? so am I." The shades of difference in meaning
between "Hebrews," "Israelites," and "the seed of Abraham" have been variously stated. Possibly the first refers
to the pride of race, the second to peculiar privileges as
the people of God, and the third to special promises of
blessing.

The next claim Paul meets is that which the false
teachers made of having some peculiar relation to Christ:
" 'Are they ministers of Christ?' (I feel like a mad man
to be making such comparisons.) I surely have more
reason for making such a claim. What hardships in
Christ's cause have they endured in comparison with
mine?" Paul gives a recital of these sufferings. They
form the evidence by which his claim to be a servant of
Christ is supported. He is showing how much he has
suffered for the sake of Christ.

He has served more faithfully by his labors, more pa-
tiently in his imprisonments, more pitifully in enduring
cruel floggings, more frequently at the risk of his life.

"Of the Jews five times received I forty stripes save
one." It is said that forty stripes was the extreme number allowed by Jewish law, and that if exceeded, the exe-
cutioner himself would be scourged; therefore only thirty-

nine were inflicted for fear of a miscount.

"Thrice was I beaten with rods." This was a form of Gentile punishment. Of the three instances, the only one elsewhere recorded is that from which Paul suffered at Philippi.

"Once was I stoned." This was at Lystra and of it there is a full account in The Acts. "Thrice I suffered shipwreck." These wrecks were in addition to the one suffered subsequently on his way to Rome. "A night and a day have I been in the deep"—probably floating on wreckage. "In journeyings often." In this connection Paul mentions eight different kinds of danger which his journeys involved: "In perils of rivers, in perils of robbers, in perils from my countrymen, in perils from the Gentiles, in perils in the city, in perils in the wilderness, in perils in the sea, in perils among false brethren."

Paul then mentioned further sufferings which demonstrate his claim to be a minister of Christ, since he has endured them for Christ's sake. "In labor and travail, in watchings often, in hunger and thirst, in fastings often, in cold and nakedness." Probably the first clause of the next sentence, "Besides those things that are without," may better be translated, "Beside other things which I pass over." There was, moreover, a supreme additional burden which pressed on him daily, namely, his "anxiety for all the churches." He felt a deep sympathy for every one of his converts. He was distressed by the doubts of the wavering. He burned with indignation at the fall of the tempted.

If it is necessary to boast, he will make it a rule to glory only in the things that display his weakness, for they show what Christ can accomplish through a feeble instrument. He calls God to witness that what he says is true.

Rather abruptly he now introduces a brief recital of his narrow escape from Damascus when "through a window" he was "let down in a basket." This experience seems rather tame and prosaic when contrasted with the tragic and dramatic sufferings he has been recounting. No one is able to explain the apparent anticlimax. It may be conjectured that this incident is mentioned as one in a list of many similar narrow escapes, or else it may be concluded that this experience made a peculiarly deep impression on Paul's mind as being his first suffering in the service of Christ. He had come to Damascus with all the pomp and pride of a distinguished representative of the Jewish supreme council and as he left the city he was compelled to slink away in the darkness like a hunted thief. Could anything have been more humiliating? Was any subsequent experience harder to endure? What one first suffers for the sake of Christ often leaves an impression quite out of proportion to the harder trials to which he subsequently submits. (Ch. 11:22-33.)

Paul still feels compelled to boast. It is necessity rather than expediency which compels him to do so. He relates a unique spiritual experience, but connects it with the endurance of pitiful physical suffering; for, unlike his enemies, he boasts only in his weakness by which the power of Christ is made manifest.

The exact character of this experience it is not possible to understand or to explain. It was evidently the most sacred hour of his life, the highest honor of his career, and he draws aside the veil only far enough for us to see that the event is so glorious, so marvelous, that to him it was utterly without parallel. In fact, it was so unlike any other experience which he had ever known that he speaks of it as though it had happened in the life of another.

"I know a man in Christ," he says, and of course it is himself who is thus described as one who found Christ to be the sphere of all his endeavors and his hopes. Paul does not know whether, at the time, the spirit and the body of this "man" were united or whether, for the time, his spirit had left the body. Whether disembodied or not, he found himself passing through vast spaces. He was "caught up even to the third heaven," "into Paradise," where God dwells, and he "heard unspeakable words, which it is not lawful for a man to utter."

It is often asked why such a rapture was granted to the apostle if he was not to be allowed to relate the things which were revealed. The answer is plain. It was for his own comfort and encouragement and inspiration, and for the consequent strengthening of countless Christians who have read his words. Other believers should not covet or expect such an ecstasy or such a mysterious rapture or such an immediate "beatific vision" of God, yet the testimony of Paul makes things which are unseen and divine more certain and more real for them. With new confidence they can believe in the revelation which he has given in his letters of truths concerning the future life and the unseen world which otherwise would have remained either unknown or far more shadowy and dim.

Paul declares that he might well glory on behalf of one so signally honored of God as he has been. Yet in and of himself he will not glory. His glorying is as one who was a mere passive recipient of divine favor, a mere undeserving object of divine grace. Of nothing which is his own will he boast, except of his own sufferings—not of his own attainments or service or labors. Yet even if he should thus boast he would not be a fool for so doing, for he would only be speaking the truth. But he will refrain, lest anyone should form a higher opinion of him than his own deeds or words may warrant.

That he may not be uplifted by pride because of the surpassing grandeur of the revelations which have been granted him, he has been "given . . . a thorn in the flesh, a messenger of Satan to buffet" him. The nature of this malady it is impossible to discover. It was not some spiritual weakness or moral temptation, as many have supposed, but a physical disease, humiliating, agonizing, incurable, so terrible, indeed, that it could be described as devilish, literally, "an angel of Satan sent to deal blow after blow upon the body of the sufferer." The word "thorn" may be translated by the term "stake," and may denote agony so excruciating as to be properly depicted by language borrowed from the barbarous custom of impaling captives or criminals by driving stakes through their quivering bodies.

Many different forms of disease have been suggested to meet the description of the apostle, but there is no sufficient evidence on which to base a conclusion. Possibly it is providential that no one knows what constituted Paul's "thorn in the flesh," for now no sufferer is prevented from supposing that his pain is in some measure like that which the great apostle endured.

In his anguish Paul cried out for relief. On three special occasions he "besought the Lord," praying earnestly that this distress "might depart" from him.

The reply did not come in the form of deliverance from pain, but of a promise of sustaining grace and the statement of a divine purpose. "And he hath said" does not mean merely, "He made reply." The tense of the verb indicates that the reply was a continuous answer, one to be accepted for Paul's whole life, and so for all the hours of agony and the desperate cries of every suffering soul. The answer was this: "My grace is sufficient for thee: for my power is made perfect in weakness."

This blessed message not merely contains a promise that such grace will be granted that the pain can be endured with patience; it also brings the assurance that divine power finds its occasion in the time of greatest human need. Paul is given to understand that the pain cannot be removed, but that through the distress and in the person of the sufferer the power of Christ is to be revealed. God had in view some greater good for Paul and some larger blessing for the world than would have come from granting the specific request. By the patient endurance which Christ made possible, and by the work Christ was accomplishing through his weak and suffering servant, witness was being borne to the power of the living Christ, and others were being led to put their trust in him.

"Most gladly therefore will I rather glory in my weaknesses," Paul concludes. He will glory in them rather than complain of them, if they are necessary and unavoidable, "that the power of Christ may rest upon" him, or may spread a tabernacle over him. The power of the living Christ overshadowed and rested upon the human sufferer like a tent, or as the cloud of glory rested upon the Tabernacle of Israel.

From this precious passage it is of course right to conclude that Christians are to pray for relief from bodily pain and to expect God to bring deliverance; but they must remember that sometimes relief is impossible and that specific requests may be denied. Every sufferer, however, may rely confidently upon divine power to give patience, and may rest assured that out of the distress his Lord will bring some abiding good, and through him manifest to others the glories of divine grace.

With such truths in mind Paul concludes that if his necessary sufferings and hardships are making Christ better known, and are thus furthering the purpose of his life, he can not only endure them but rejoice in them. "Wherefore I take pleasure," writes the apostle, "in weaknesses, in injuries, in necessities, in persecutions, in distresses, for Christ's sake: for when I am weak, then am I strong." He has learned in the school of suffering that the times of greatest weakness and of utter dependence upon Christ are those in which his presence is most fully realized and service for him is most effective.

D. THE SIGNS OF AN APOSTLE
Ch. 12:11-18

11 I am become foolish: ye compelled me; for I ought to have been commended of you: for in nothing was I behind the very chiefest apostles, though I am nothing. 12 Truly the signs of an apostle were wrought among you in

*all patience, by signs and wonders and mighty works. 13
For what is there wherein ye were made inferior to the rest
of the churches, except* it be *that I myself was not a burden
to you? forgive me this wrong.*

*14 Behold, this is the third time I am ready to come to
you; and I will not be a burden to you: for I seek not
yours, but you: for the children ought not to lay up for
the parents, but the parents for the children. 15 And I will
most gladly spend and be spent for your souls. If I love
you more abundantly, am I loved the less? 16 But be it so,
I did not myself burden you; but, being crafty, I caught
you with guile. 17 Did I take advantage of you by any one
of them whom I have sent unto you? 18 I exhorted Titus,
and I sent the brother with him. Did Titus take any advantage of you? walked we not in the same spirit?* walked
we *not in the same steps?*

Paul has concluded his boasting. It has been absolutely
necessary. His opponents have compelled him to adopt a
method of defense which he declares to be foolish. By
their arrogant claims they have been stealing away the
hearts of his disciples. They have been imperiling the
church of Christ. Paul has been forced to defend his
apostolic authority against the boasting of these false
apostles and to meet their cruel charge that he is an impostor. He has shown that in his labors for Christ, but
more particularly in his sufferings for Christ, he has been
demonstrated to be a true servant of his Lord; and he
has made all the claims of his opponents seem absolutely
absurd.

Yet, as he concludes this section of enforced boasting,
he declares that his friends at Corinth who have been
beguiled by these false teachers are themselves at fault
in this matter of his necessary self-defense. "I am become
foolish," he writes, "ye compelled me; for I ought to have
been commended of you." They should have been the
ones to protect the apostle. They should have made it
unnecessary for him to write in his own behalf. They
should have known that he alone had grounds for boasting.

They had in hand abundant evidence for refuting the proud claims and the impertinent charges of his enemies. They knew the truth of the statement which follows, as he insists with severe sarcasm: "For in nothing was I behind those precious apostles of yours, those preeminent apostles, though indeed I am nothing."

That his authority was genuine and real, the Corinthians should have had no doubt: "Truly the signs of an apostle were wrought among you in all patience, by signs and wonders and mighty works." The credentials of which Paul reminds his readers had been placed before them in the works which he wrought in their midst. There had been his self-sacrificing toil and labor, and moreover, those miracles which attended and authenticated the mission of every true apostle of Christ. The test of an apostle was not only the absolute requirement of having seen the risen Lord, but further, the ability to perform those supernatural wonders by which Paul's own divine mission had been attested. Paul always claimed to possess such credentials, and apparently he had never exhibited them more impressively than in the presence of the Corinthian church. They, therefore, of all believers, should have been the last to doubt his official authority, and should have been ready at once to meet every charge which was preferred against him.

He asks, with withering sarcasm, if there is any particular in which he has shown to the Corinthians any reason for doubting his authority as an apostle, which all the other churches of Christ are recognizing. There is, he admits, one point in which they "were made inferior to the rest of the churches." It is in the fact that he had refused to burden them with his financial support. For this great fault and slight he begs them to grant him pardon: "Forgive me this wrong." (Vs. 11-13.)

There was another sign of Paul's sincerity, another proof that his commission was genuine. It was found in the love which he showed toward the members of the Corinthian church. This had been manifest in many ways, but most specifically in his unselfish refusal to burden them with any financial remuneration for his labors. His work had fully demonstrated his apostleship, but for it he had accepted no return. The custom which he had previously adopted was to be continued on the visit which he was about to make.

He reminds them that this will be his third visit to them. On the occasion of his first visit he founded the church and brought it to a position of great strength. Of his second visit we have no definite record. It is commonly supposed to have been brief and painful. This second epistle was written to prepare the Corinthians for his coming, so that he would be spared a repetition of his former distress, and would find them ready to receive him with gladness and affection. He therefore reminded them of the love which he had always borne toward them. It was the love of a father for his spiritual children. He had brought them to Christ and so had given them the experience of a new and higher life. It was because he felt for them such affection that he was again refusing to accept any support at their hands. He was ready to give his very life to them, but he was not willing to accept gifts from them until he was absolutely certain of their love. "For the children ought not to lay up for the parents, but the parents for the children," he writes. "And I will most gladly spend and be spent for your souls."

Should not such self-sacrifice be rewarded by trust and affection? Should it be used by Paul's enemies as a ground for arousing suspicion of his genuineness: "If I love you more abundantly, am I loved the less?" "But my enemies are suggesting," he says, "that even though I did not receive any financial support from you, I shrewdly managed to obtain your money through the messengers whom I sent. I did not myself burden you; but by being crafty I caught you with guile."

By "them whom I have sent unto you" Paul means those who had been sent by him to complete the collection for

the poor saints in Jerusalem. It appears from this statement that his contemptible enemies endeavored to undermine the confidence of the Corinthians in him, not only by
stating that he did not dare to accept a salary, but even by
the mean insinuation that there was something very suspicious about this collection which he was making, and
that there was much probability that in this reputed offering Paul had a secret personal interest.

To this cruel slander he replies with some spirit, by asking whether it is true, and by challenging his readers to
point to any fact in the conduct of his representatives which
might support such a cruel charge. "Did I take advantage
of you by any one of them whom I have sent unto you? I
exhorted Titus, and I sent the brother with him. Did Titus
take any advantage of you? walked we not in the same
spirit? walked we not in the same steps?" By this series
of questions Paul reminds his readers of the course of unselfish service which he and his delegates have followed.
From first to last, Paul's dealings with the Corinthians had
shown only devotion and self-forgetfulness and love. Was
there any reason for doubting him or for questioning the
fact that he was a genuine apostle of Christ?

After all, what are the truest credentials of a Christian,
and specifically, of a public messenger of Christ? Are they
not service, self-sacrifice, and love? And have these ever
been exhibited more fully and more genuinely than by the
apostle Paul?

E. THE FINAL WARNINGS   Chs. 12:19 to 13:10

*19 Ye think all this time that we are excusing ourselves
unto you. In the sight of God speak we in Christ. But all
things, beloved,* are *for your edifying. 20 For I fear, lest
by any means, when I come, I should find you not such as
I would, and should myself be found of you such as ye
would not; lest by any means there should be* strife, jealousy, wraths, factions, backbitings, whisperings, swellings,
tumults; *21 lest again when I come my God should hum-*

ble me before you, and I should mourn for many of them that have sinned heretofore, and repented not of the uncleanness and fornication and lasciviousness which they committed.

1 This is the third time I am coming to you. At the mouth of two witnesses or three shall every word be established. 2 I have said beforehand, and I do say beforehand, as when I was present the second time, so now, being absent, to them that have sinned heretofore, and to all the rest, that, if I come again, I will not spare; 3 seeing that ye seek a proof of Christ that speaketh in me; who to youward is not weak, but is powerful in you: 4 for he was crucified through weakness, yet he liveth through the power of God. For we also are weak in him, but we shall live with him through the power of God toward you. 5 Try your own selves, whether ye are in the faith; prove your own selves. Or know ye not as to your own selves, that Jesus Christ is in you? unless indeed ye be reprobate. 6 But I hope that ye shall know that we are not reprobate. 7 Now we pray to God that ye do no evil; not that we may appear approved, but that ye may do that which is honorable, though we be as reprobate. 8 For we can do nothing against the truth, but for the truth. 9 For we rejoice, when we are weak, and ye are strong: this we also pray for, even your perfecting. 10 For this cause I write these things while absent, that I may not when present deal sharply, according to the authority which the Lord gave me for building up, and not for casting down.

Paul concludes the passionate defense of his apostolic authority with a series of solemn warnings. These are in view of his approaching visit to Corinth. Unless there is repentance and reformation on the part of the Corinthians, he will find it necessary to demonstrate his apostolic authority by exercising severe discipline. He hopes that such a course will be unnecessary. On his second brief visit his forbearance seems to have been misinterpreted as weakness. This will not happen again. The power which he is claiming in this letter will be demonstrated by the severity of his action.

In referring to his defense, which he is here concluding, he declares that his purpose has not been to vindicate himself, but to secure their spiritual profit: "Ye think all this time that we are excusing ourselves unto you." He would not have them so conclude. He does not want them to suppose that he has been arguing his case before them as his judges. On the contrary, since he is speaking as a servant of Christ and under the guidance of his Spirit, God alone is his judge: "In the sight of God speak we in Christ." What he has been seeking is the strengthening and the upbuilding of their Christian characters. "All things, beloved, are for your edifying."

He is anxious lest on his arrival he should find them impenitent and obstinate and so should be compelled to show a severity by which they might be distressed: "For I fear, lest by any means, when I come, I should find you not such as I would, and should myself be found of you such as ye would not."

He feared lest he might find them guilty of the sins of self-will and self-indulgence which were threatening to destroy the church. Among the former class of evils he mentions "strife, jealousy, wraths, factions, backbitings, whisperings, swellings, tumults." "Backbitings" and "whisperings" probably refer to open and to secret defaming of character. "Swellings" denote acts of pride and insolence, while "tumults" probably indicate the disturbances in the church which might result from the faults enumerated.

The second list of faults refers more particularly to those sins of the flesh and of gross immorality against which all dwellers in Corinth needed to be warned. The apostle fears lest when he reaches the city he may again be humiliated and compelled to mourn over those who have not repented of their former sins, which on his previous visit he had rebuked. Whatever other experience had distressed the apostle, he refers here to the shame he had felt at finding professed converts of his falling into such a depth of moral degradation.

He enforces this call to repentance by an assurance that he will soon be with them and that then he will administer discipline with justice but with due severity: "This is the third time I am coming to you. At the mouth of two witnesses or three shall every word be established." This reference from the Old Testament is probably introduced to emphasize the certainty and the searching judicial character of the punishment which he will inflict. He warned them against evil ways when on his former visit, and now again he gives warning, not only to the former offenders but to any others who may have lapsed into sin: "I have said beforehand, . . . as when I was present the second time, so now, being absent, to them that have sinned heretofore, and to all the rest, that, if I come again, I will not spare."

Since they are demanding some evidence that he is speaking as an apostle of Christ, if they make it necessary, he will give them a demonstration even though it is not of a kind which they could enjoy. They had been given proofs that the power of Christ was working through Paul. These were found in the very creation of the Corinthian church and in the bestowal of those spiritual gifts of which the Corinthian Christians were proud. So Paul could say, "Christ that speaketh in me; . . . to you-ward is not weak, but is powerful in you." This Christ was indeed "crucified through weakness," experiencing the humiliation of death, "yet he liveth through the power of God." He is working through his apostles with divine energy. So it is with Paul. He may have seemed weak when on a previous visit he showed forbearance and gentleness. On his next arrival he will show the Corinthians by the severity of his discipline that he is one through whom the living Christ is manifesting his divine power: "For we also are weak in him, but we shall live with him through the power of God toward you." He urges them to test themselves, rather than to be asking for proofs of his apostolic power. They might better be asking what assurance they have that they are Christians: "Try your own selves, whether ye are in the faith; prove your own selves."

He asks them whether they have possibly forgotten that Christ is dwelling in them, even this very Christ whom they have offended and who will be certain through his apostle to show his displeasure and to give any needed rebuke. He assures them that Christ does indeed dwell in them unless they are "reprobate" or false Christians. He hopes that they will discover under the guidance of Christ that he is not a false apostle as some have charged. He makes his earnest prayer to God that they may do no evil thing. This is not merely that they may prove a credit to him and may thus attest the genuineness of his apostolic mission, but it is with the hope that their course may be "honorable" and worthy and noble. He is eager to have this prayer answered even though it should take from him the possibility of proving his apostleship by administering necessary discipline, even though this lack should leave him in this sense disapproved, or, as he says, "Though we be as reprobate."

"For we can do nothing against the truth, but for the truth." This does not mean that all opposition to truth is futile. However accurate such a statement may be, it is far from the thought which Paul is intending to express. He means to say that as an apostle of Christ it would be impossible for him to desire or to wish to find any occasion of disciplining the Corinthians merely to demonstrate his own authority and power. To rejoice in evil because it gave him an advantage of any kind would be morally impossible for Paul. "He cannot desire that they should be found to be doing wrong in order that he may be proved to be right."

He continues to explain: "We rejoice, when we are weak, and ye are strong." That is to say, he is not only willing to have no opportunity of displaying his power in inflicting discipline, but he delights in such a condition, for it means that the Corinthians "are strong" in their spiritual life and in their moral steadfastness. He adds emphatically, "This we also pray for, even your perfecting." There has been nothing selfish in Paul's course. His whole desire has been the well-being and the spiritual growth of his converts. His defense of his authority and his opposition to his enemies have been with a view to the welfare of the church, and he explains that such is the specific purpose of this epistle. He desires to secure the repentance of the Corinthians and to avoid the necessity of inflicting discipline. He has been entrusted with apostolic power for the edification and not the destruction of these Corinthian believers: "For this cause I write these things while absent, that I may not when present deal sharply, according to the authority which the Lord gave me for building up, and not for casting down."

IV
THE CONCLUSION
Ch. 13:11-14

11 Finally, brethren, farewell. Be perfected; be com-
forted; be of the same mind; live in peace: and the God of
love and peace shall be with you. 12 Salute one another
with a holy kiss.
13 All the saints salute you.
14 The grace of the Lord Jesus Christ, and the love of
God, and the communion of the Holy Spirit, be with you
all.

The storm of passion is over, and Paul breathes upon
his followers a last word of affectionate counsel, a salutation, and a prayer. He has warned the wayward and has
rebuked the impenitent, but he includes all in the circle
of his love, as he calls them his "brethren." He regards
all believers as forming one great family of God. It is
indeed the most famous and beneficent fraternity in the
world.

To all his brotherhood Paul sends his word of closing
greeting: "Finally, brethren, farewell," or, more literally,
"rejoice." Neither word alone fully expresses the idea of
the apostle. The last term was a natural close for a
Greek letter and was about equivalent to our modern con-
ventional "good-by." Yet in the letters of Paul it is used
in the sense of "rejoice." Here "rejoice" is too strong and
definite. Possibly both meanings may be included: "Let
my last word to you be to rejoice."

"Be perfected," or press on to perfection. There is
much to be amended; many grave faults have been committed; there are many deficiencies to be made good. Per-
severe. Seek the highest spiritual attainment.

"Be comforted." Comfort and counsel translate the
same word, and here the sense may be, "Listen to my

exhortations; obey what I have told you.   Real comfort will thus be secured."

"Be of the same mind."   No body of Christians was more in need of this exhortation than the Corinthian church.   It may well be repeated to every group of believers today.   The result of obedience to this command is the ability to "live in peace"; but there is an even more blessed consequence: "The God of love and peace shall be with you."

"The God of love" is a phrase found only here; "the God of peace" is frequent in Paul's writings.   John writes that "God is love," and the New Testament ever teaches that love and peace are among the chief of God's perfect gifts.

As Paul urges his readers to "salute one another with a holy kiss," he refers to the common symbol of Christian brotherhood; the observance of this form in the church assembly would be an expression of the love and peace which the Corinthians so seriously lacked.

It was gracious of the apostle to add, "All the saints salute you."   Although his rebukes have been severe, he here assures his readers that all his fellow Christians recognize the standing of the Corinthian church as composed of those who belong to Christ and are being sanctified in him.

The letter closes with what has become commonly known as the apostolic benediction.   It is the fullest form of benediction used by Paul and appears rather significantly at the close of his most severe letter.

Here Father, Son, and Holy Ghost are addressed as one in this comprehensive fervent petition.   The unmerited favor of Christ, the boundless love of God, the fellowship of the Holy Spirit, are invoked upon all the members of the turbulent, restless Corinthian church; and they can be confidently claimed today by everyone who belongs to the universal body of Christ, the church of the living God, the "communion of saints."